IN THE PROVINCE OF BIRDS

IN THE PROVINCE OF BIRDS
A MEMOIR FROM WESTERN ARKANSAS

Joseph C. Neal

Half Acre Press
Fayetteville ■ 2011

Copyright © 2011 by Joseph C. Neal

All rights reserved
Manufactured in the United States of America

ISBN: 978-0-9829455-5-1

All photographs by Joseph C. Neal except where noted

Designed by Liz Lester

Preferred citation:
Neal, Joseph C. 2011. *In the Province of Birds (A Memoir of Western Arkansas).*
Half Acre Press, Fayetteville AR. 210 pp.

frontispiece photo: Joe Neal carrying his spotting scope at Baker Prairie Natural Area in Harrison, Arkansas, on May 28, 2011. *Photo by David Oakley.*

HALF
ACRE
PRESS
www.halfacrepress.com

CONTENTS

Preface	vii
Winter Trip to Horn Island	1
Cave Mountain	21
Charlie	37
Yard Birds	49
Rolling Knolls	65
Richard	83
God's Second Bible	93
The Golden Calf	111
November	131
Woodpecker Business	147
Digiscoping Hawks and Eagles	167
Yellow-billed Loon	183

Abandoned house on the former Wet Prairie near Maysville, Arkansas, on February 13, 2011.

PREFACE

The Acorn Doesn't Fall Far from the Tree

FIVE THOUSAND PRIMARILY mountainous square miles in western Arkansas comprises my personal geography. My family history lies almost entirely within this landscape. It's roughly one hundred miles north to south and half that east to west. Southern Missouri is my North Country. Eastern Oklahoma is my Far West. The Buffalo River headwaters of Newton County are Back East. In the South, I'm at home in the Ouachita Mountains. Bigger than a city, smaller than a state, it's a province of sorts.

My mother, Hazel Kennedy Neal, anchors my south. She was born in 1917 and reared on a Ouachita Mountain farm in Logan County near Magazine. Much of her family lies south of Magazine in the graveyard adjacent to the Lick Creek church, an attractive space of family stories, tilting headstones, short grass, and large trees. I hear Chipping Sparrows near the Kennedy plot. My great-great-aunt Effie Van Allen, for example, died in the big flu epidemic of 1919. My great-grandpa Ben Kennedy died in a fight over a hog in 1924. His big, now tilting headstone is near the red oak where Summer Tanagers nest. It couldn't have been much more than an acorn the year he passed.

My father, Grover Ray Neal, was born and reared in the Arkansas River town of Van Buren, across from Fort Smith. This is roughly in the center of my province. We had lots of Sunday after-church dinners at Granny (Jessie Hanson) Neal's place. This was in the 1950s, when Sunday-noon, pan-fried chicken, homemade yeast rolls, white gravy, and cherry pie palliated the moral tonic of Southern Baptist Sunday morning exhortation. After dinner I was free to roam Van Buren.

Jessie Hanson Neal (left) with Grover and Hazel Neal, off to church in 1955. *From the collection of the Neal family.*

I wish I could report that at that tender age I closely studied the birds of the Arkansas River, especially the colonies of endangered interior Least Terns. Wouldn't that make a great beginning for a collection of birding essays? But, alas, I was really just walking off a full belly. However, this Lord's Day afternoon habit of roaming and random investigation would eventually lead to wider investigations like those recounted in the following essays.

My mother's parents, Ernest and Estelle (Franklin) Kennedy, lost their Lick Creek farm in 1929 during the Great Depression. They moved to Fort Smith, where my mother was reared. My grandfather gave up farming for a paycheck, steady but modest, from the scissors factory down by the Poteau River, where it flows into the Arkansas. That's near the infamous Judge Parker gallows. Grandmother gardened, canned, milked the cow, and starched-up everyone for Sunday at Emmanuel Baptist. They owned a pump organ, but never a car.

My dad's father Grover Cleveland Neal operated a grocery on Main

Street in Van Buren, a few blocks above the Arkansas River. GC was a kind man who gave shoes to poor children, played cards, and drank beer throughout Prohibition. Granny Neal was a devout Presbyterian and renowned Sunday-school teacher. GC died of leukemia in 1943 midst World War II.

My father, who had enlisted in the navy in December 1941 after Pearl Harbor, was granted an emergency shore leave for the funeral. My folks met at that time.

The western-Arkansas Neals date back to the territorial period. The first families came up the Arkansas River as scouts in the late 1820s, accompanying Cherokees and other Native Americans who were then being forced to immigrate into Indian Territory, now Oklahoma, not even a mile west as Fish Crows fly from Van Buren and Fort Smith. These early Neals settled on rich native grassland between Alma and Van Buren. It was once called Neal's Prairie. I presume they made short work of the Greater Prairie-Chickens. They were as welcome at the table those days as fried chicken at Granny Neal's.

My mother's Kennedy relatives immigrated into Arkansas somewhat later. One of my great-great-relatives, Robert Kennedy, was wounded during the Civil War. He never recovered and passed about 1867 at Paris, Texas. From Texas, the family trekked through southeastern Oklahoma across the Ouachitas into western Arkansas. Along the way three Kennedy brothers met and married three Hokit sisters. Eventually, several families settled in Logan County, Arkansas, probably in the 1870s and became Lick Creek farmers. My grandfather Ernest was born there in 1896.

My grandmother Estelle Kennedy's family, the Franklins, were railroaders from northern Alabama. They moved to the Ouachitas to help build the Rock Island Railroad in the 1880s. The Rock Island Line was "Main Street" in the central Ouachitas. The old right-of-way is never far from Highway 10, down through the Ouachitas heartland of central Arkansas. Franklins hauled and hammered down massive bridge timbers you can still see along the highway.

Eventually my mother's grandfather, Ben Kennedy, made his money herding hogs. He became a prosperous landowner in the Lick Creek area of Logan County and served for a time as Magazine mayor. Old

Ernest and Estelle Kennedy with baby Hazel at Magazine, Arkansas in 1917. *From the collection of the Neal family.*

Ben Kennedy fattened his hogs in the acorn-rich river bottom woods of Lick Creek and the Petit Jean River. I too have "called the hogs," but it was three generations after old Ben, and not in the Lick Creek valley, but rather as a University of Arkansas student (they still "call the Hogs" at Razorback athletic games). Continuing in this family tradition, I'm also interested in acorns, though these days it usually involves watching Blue Jays and Red-headed Woodpeckers carrying them to secret caches.

These Kennedys and railroading Franklins must also have helped to cut the virgin shortleaf pine timber on the ridges above their places in

Kennedy place on Lick Creek in the Ouachita Mountains. *From the collection of the Neal family.*

the Ouachita Mountains. I've never heard that any of them were birders, so they probably didn't know much about the now highly endangered Red-cockaded Woodpecker. These woodpeckers excavate sap wells in the big pines. The excavations or "rosin wells" ooze large amount of sticky, turpentine smelling sap that can repel snakes that climb the trees to eat young woodpeckers. The heavily sapped trees are distinctive even to nonbirders. The Kennedys and Franklins in my blood probably recognized the "turpentine trees" associated with this now rare bird.

I gratefully acknowledge my sister, Ruth Lloyd Hope of Atlanta, Georgia. She is a great supporter of me, her "little" brother. Most importantly here, she has memories of our Kennedy and Franklin families that she shared with me.

Most of the old piney woods of Logan County are now part of the Ouachita National Forest. It is within the realm of irony that a native son, me, returned to the old home country more than a century after the Kennedys moved to Logan County. That's me out there in the green uniform. I'm working on the National Forest to protect and hopefully recover the small remaining populations of Red-cockaded Woodpeckers.

Sisters on a new bike, Billie Ruth (Hope) in front and sister Jerrie (Kirk) in the late 1940s. *From the collection of the Neal family.*

I realize that the nuts and bolts of these lineages and family names are confusing. Take heart: it's also confusing for me. There's a Bates community in western Scott County and a Bates Cemetery in Waldron, and these are connected somehow to Granny Neal's mother, Mary P. Bates. But how, exactly? My family members are buried in Fayetteville, Cedarville, Van Buren, Fort Smith (two cemeteries), Greenwood, Casa, Lick Creek, and somewhere on the Paris side of Magazine Mountain—that's just the ones I know about. Point is, this neck of the woods in western Arkansas is a personal province. Local people say the acorn doesn't fall far from the tree. That seems to be the case with me.

I live in Fayetteville in the western Arkansas Ozarks, a city in my provincial north. I have the grasslands and former prairies of the Springfield Plateau. The rugged, heavily forested Boston Mountains spread before my eyes. The city of Fort Smith and the Arkansas River Valley form my central tableau. The great ridges and valleys of shortleaf pine and hardwoods in the Ouachita Mountains dominate my south. Beyond lies terra incognita.

My Main Street is Old Highway 71, now largely replaced by I-540. Back in the 1920s and 1930s, the highway now called 71 replaced another Main Street, the Frisco Railroad. And to be fair, in the 1880s, railroads such as the Frisco replaced wagon trails and footpaths of pioneer hunters and Native Americans.

Modern I-540 is beautiful and easy to drive. It dazzles travelers with a grand tunnel, soaring vistas of the Boston Mountains, and deep streams with bridges that are wonders of engineering. Yet, I have not taken joy in the enormous ecological damage done Ozark forests and streams by its construction. I have derived great benefit from its presence, but awareness of its overall impact is at least somewhere on my mind. That said, I race along at seventy-plus miles an hour like everyone else trying to make a living. I accept the contradiction in my twin role as commuter and conservationist. I have not changed my mind about convenience's hidden costs.

Fayetteville was once the main town in the north, but Fayetteville, Springdale, Rogers, and Bentonville have become Northwest Arkansas City, stretching twenty-five miles from north to south. Fort Smith is hub for, at the very least, Alma, Van Buren, Greenwood. Maybe this can be called Western Arkansas City.

The concrete and asphalt of these urban hubs cover former Tallgrass Prairies, attractive to pioneers because they lacked barriers to farming and transportation. Today our cattle herds fatten on fescue grasses replacing native bluestem grasses. Small patches of true prairie remain in Benton County and Carroll County in the north and in Sebastian and Franklin Counties in the south. Native birds that require prairie grasslands have predictably declined.

My drives through western Arkansas traverse the rugged forested Ouachitas and Ozarks, including the Boston Mountains. There are two vast public-land holdings here, the Ozark-St. Francis National Forest and the Ouachita National Forest.

In the north, the Ozark-St Francis totals over one million acres of public lands. Many bird species declining elsewhere remain relatively healthy here. Colorful birds like Scarlet Tanagers are common. Cerulean Warblers, which have suffered big declines elsewhere, can be found during summer in scattered but predictable stands of mature hardwood trees with a rich understory of native plants, including the strange and mysterious pawpaws.

Stretching into eastern Oklahoma, the Ouachita's two million acres make it the largest National Forest in the eastern United States.

In 2002, this abandoned and partially stripped truck was associated with an old homestead in what is today Mount Sequoyah Woods Park in Fayetteville.

Northern slopes are dominated by mixed hardwood species, south slopes by shortleaf pine. One of its many treasures is a small, but slowly recovering population of Red-cockaded Woodpeckers.

Headwaters of the upper Buffalo National River are about one hour east of my home in Fayetteville. Citizens successfully fought developers and government who sought to bury the free-flowing river under a dam in the 1960s and early 1970s. These citizen efforts ensure this legacy will grace and inspire future generations.

The grand old Arkansas River loops around Fort Smith and then heads southeast toward the Mississippi. Dams on the Arkansas have created impoundments and new unnatural (but interesting) habitats for gulls, pelicans, cormorants, and big rafts of ducks. We have lost the old river, and gained a whole new bird community. I think about this contradiction as I scan flocks of Bonaparte's Gulls for a lone Little Gull.

Southeast of Fort Smith is a vast military reservation, Fort Chaffee, including prairie grasslands. The military didn't convert the old prairies to fescue pastures. Artillery shells instead maintained these grasslands in the old fashioned way, with wildfires, much as in presettlement times. Bell's Vireos are common in summer and Smith's Longspurs are often present in winter. Thus have the needs of war preserved a natural aspect of our past. This irony is not lost on me, though I don't always understand how such apparently disparate pieces of a vast puzzle fit together.

Taken together, these many elements form a core for my personal landscape. I encompass contradictions on a cosmic scale. I welcome them.

These essays have consumed me in various forms since the 1970s. They have slowly evolved in various feature stories, published and unpublished.

I want to express my gratitude to the family of artist Walter Inglis Anderson of Ocean Springs, Mississippi, for their kindnesses during many trips to the Gulf Coast in the late 1970s and early 1980s. I got my official start as a birder among them on Horn Island—about as fine a province of birds as one could imagine.

The now defunct *Grapevine* in Fayetteville published early versions of several essays in the late 1970s and 1980s. Various editors encouraged me over the years—Doug and Brynda Howard, Peter Tooker, and Nancy Maier. Basically, they opened the paper's pages to me, as well as other writers, allowing us to write what we felt, and along the way to get the feel of writing for an audience.

Arkansas Wildlife, a publication of the Arkansas Game and Fish Commission, published several of my bird stories, including two on Red-cockaded Woodpeckers and another about the shorebirds that migrate through the state fish hatchery at Centerton.

I also tried out several ideas that would evolve into longer essays in the pages of the *Fayetteville Free Weekly.*

My colleagues on the Ouachita National Forest have accepted and often supported my birding interests. I worked for years especially with Keith Piles and Warren Montague on Poteau Ranger District at Waldron. On the adjoining Cold Springs Ranger District, it was my pleasure to share work with Frances Rothwein and Nelva Bohannan. Their interests and personalities have rubbed off on me.

Doug James has been a long time friend, mentor, birding companion, and my coauthor on *Arkansas Birds.* Doug freely shares with me his enthusiasm for many things in life—barn-storming birding trips to Texas, the Breeding Bird Survey, Christmas Bird Count, and the Arkansas Audubon Society, late night conversation over beer, to name a few. I could not have written these and other essays without the benefit of these shared experiences now exceeding thirty years. Field trips and other adventures recounted in the following pages have also been shared with Kimberly G. Smith, in the University of Arkansas Department of Biological Sciences.

In the early 1980s, not long after I met Mike Mlodinow, we decided to explore birds of the Illinois River in my new canoe. We promptly ran into some underwater concrete, parts of a disused bridge. The sudden jolt swamped the canoe. Mike's glasses disappeared and an enormous bruise rose on my leg where I slammed a thwart. We were younger then. We journeyed on to Warbling Vireos, Prothonotary Warblers, and other interesting birds that day. We are still finding birds of interest. He inspires all of us in the Arkansas birding community with careful analysis of data and attention to difficult identification problems.

Irene Marie Anne Camargo and I made noontime outings to view ducks at the Fayetteville sewer-plant ponds. Munch, munch, munch—down goes lunch. We scan the pond, balancing between sandwiches and spotting scope. Munch, munch. Look at all of those scaup! Wow! It's a great place to observe divers. That's a flock of Hooded Mergansers! Thanks for that and for the card sent years ago from the Tallgrass Prairie Preserve in Osage County, Oklahoma.

Like Doug and Mike, the artist Richard Stauffacher has been a companion on many field trips—birds, flowers, frogs, and recording sessions with bluegrass music at the Brentwood Community Center. Richard is a careful artist and a careful reader. This is what he wrote to me about some earlier essays: "Joseph Campbell says 'the form is secondary—the important thing is the message, a message concerning the relationship between time and eternal powers.' Walter Anderson talks about the relationship between 'spirit and matter,' and that's what all his work is about. So you want my advice? Make all your writing 'a message concerning the relationship between time and eternal powers.' Any piece of art or literature that doesn't pick the viewer up and deposit him or her in the presence of some eternal power is a dud."

Joe Neal on the steps of Granny Henderson's cabin in the Buffalo National River. *Photograph by Richard Stauffacher in September 2006.*

I am grateful to book designer and Half Acre Press publisher, Liz Lester, who read through enough of my stuff to see its value as a book (or actually books) and commenced the process that got us here. She also brought copy editor Brian King into this process. I thought I knew how to punctuate and spell before Brian, but his work on *The Birdside Baptist* (published in 2010) unified and improved my often-uneven prose. Now I can read the book without wincing at my grammatical mistakes. In my opinion, he has repeated the magic here.

My friend Eleanor Lincoln Johnson passed away as I was finishing this book, just short of her one-hundredth birthday. Ellie supported me as a writer, birder, gardener, and father. She was godmother to my daughter, Ariel. Ellie liked to get things done, especially things that made the world livable, and not livable just for those with enough cash to buy off life's harsh edges. She wrote letters to keep dams off the

Buffalo River, hired plumbers to help elderly shut-ins who couldn't afford to repair broken water lines. Her other ministries included the local animal shelter, juvenile runaways, and delivering home-cooked meals ("meals on wheels") in her VW bug. We sat many an hour in white plastic chairs in her yard, drinking coffee and enjoying her flowers and the sunshine near Razorback Stadium.

I hereby lift a cup in toast to the spirits of those like Ellie who see our world, not as burden, but as opportunity. Remember, it's not about the cash. At least some of it is for the birds.

Winter Trip
to Horn Island

ON A JUNE evening in 1977 I boarded a Trailways bus in Fayetteville, Arkansas. Twenty hours and six hundred miles later, I was at Biloxi on the Mississippi Gulf Coast. I was on a mission to discover Walter Inglis Anderson, or at least explore his legend. It was one of those burning afternoons when the sky is stuffed with cumulus clouds and the Gulf is a sheet of blinding glass. My destination was Ocean Springs, five miles east across Biloxi Bay.

I was thirty-one that year and did not own a car. It was not that I just didn't own one. I did not "believe" in cars. I don't mean it in the same way as not believing in flying saucers. My values included clean skies, wild creatures, and no oil wars. I couldn't see how there was room for those values AND cars. Cars were at best a convenience of Faustian proportion. Thirty-one isn't a bad time to test beliefs and alternatives.

I knew something of Ocean Springs and its famous resident from a book entitled *The Horn Island Logs of Walter Inglis Anderson*. He traveled on foot, bicycle, and skiff in order to sketch, paint, and write about the Gulf Coast's wild creatures. He married and fathered children. He spent weeks working alone on uninhabited islands. At times he suffered mental illness. He was something of a recluse when he died in 1965. His cottage was full of drawings and paintings that today are acknowledged as masterpieces.

Horn Island is one of several sandy barriers protecting mainland Mississippi from storms blowing in from the Gulf. At about fourteen miles long, three-fourths of a mile at its widest, Horn totals under four thousand acres—depending upon sand gained and sand lost from the latest hurricane. It's barely ten miles offshore.

Pine trees form part of the landscape of Horn Island, now a wilderness area in the Gulf Islands National Seashore. Protecting the mainland during hurricanes, Horn is blasted by high winds and storm-driven waves.

Redding Sugg Jr., the book's editor, believed that Anderson's life demonstrated "a concrete witness and proof that man can relate to wilderness on its own terms and get munificent personal rewards from the relationship." I was intrigued that Anderson focused on intimate natural history—birds, crabs, fish, flowers, his children at play, his wife reading. Anderson seemed to me independent of, or perhaps indifferent to, modern society. I was feeling that way myself.

I jumped off the bus at Biloxi, loaded my gear on my back, and hiked along the highway toward the Biloxi Bay bridge and Ocean Springs, which had no bus depot. I wilted immediately. Twenty hours on an air-conditioned bus was no preparation for the coast. In Ocean Springs I found a bench under a massive live oak whose roots disrupted and protruded from the concrete, its shade spreading across the street.

A former train station had been made into a visitor's center. I met a young woman who soon introduced me to Mary Stebly, Walter Anderson's daughter. I feared my outfit of ragged shorts, beard, and scuffed tennis shoes might not make a best first impression. I was soon put at ease. Mary herself was wearing paint-speckled jeans. She painted signs for the Ocean Springs Little Theatre, entertained her two youngest sons with casual banter, and talked to me too.

Mary knew a hungry pilgrim when she saw one. I was invited for lunch. Afterwards, the boys rounded up fishing gear, and we walked one block to Mary's childhood home, Shearwater Pottery. The turn-off was marked by a neatly painted Black Skimmer, the boldly patterned black-and-white sea bird that flies close to the water's surface, shearing it with their elongated, reddish lower beak while scooping up fish.

The pottery occupies twenty-four forested acres fronting the Mississippi Sound and the barrier islands, including Horn. A big frame house dating to the 1830s was home for Walter's brother Peter and Peter's family. There were also newer homes of various Anderson children and a unique rammed-earth home built by Walter's brother James.

An old bicycle learned against the weathered boards of an open frame building dwarfed by massive loblolly pines: welcome to the Shearwater workshops. The weathered framed structures fitted comfortably into the landscape of coastal marsh and lowland forest. They seemed an outgrowth, rather than a conquest, of the surrounding landscape. The soft hum and slap of a machine sounded through screenless windows. Inside, Mary introduced me to her uncle Peter Anderson, Walter's older brother. Peter established the pottery in the 1928. He offered a handshake, polite comments about the weather and the value of barometers. Then he handed me clay. Would I like to throw?

A short walk up the drive brought us to the showroom. Pottery, paintings, prints, woodcarvings, and other artistic productions of the Andersons and related families were offered for sale. I met James "Mac" Anderson, the youngest of the three brothers. Like his siblings, Mac was a painter and designer of vision and accomplishment. "Standardization facilitates marketing," he said, "but we feel standardization to any great extent would sacrifice the individuality and variety of our handiwork."

Across the road from the showroom I was introduced to Mary's mother and Walter Anderson's wife, Agnes Grinstead Anderson, Sissy to family and friends. She had just turned seventy and was retired from a long career that included many years of teaching first graders plus raising her own four children.

She lived in the "barn," a frame structure of well-seasoned lumber

Sissy Anderson walking on Horn Island in January 1979. She took great pleasure exploring the island as she was working on a book about life with her now-famous artist husband.

and many windows. It had been converted from its original purpose to a house of a size and informality to accommodate a growing family. Gulf weather is mild most of the year. Various openings in walls and windows admit the busy presence of nature. Sissy mentioned raccoons that she accepted as winter residents in the attic. I noticed, too, that she permitted curious vines to enter her bedroom via openings above the windows.

Many are the pilgrims drawn to the romantic story of Walter Anderson's artistic life. But, as I had already learned from *The Horn Island Logs,* one troublesome aspect concerns how artistic needs and bouts of emotional instability separated him from what might be termed "a normal life." This left largely in Sissy's care many of the usual joys and burdens of family.

Walter Anderson had made regular passages between Horn Island and Ocean Springs during his final twenty years. Between these trips he lived alone in a cottage near the barn. The family called him Bob. "Bob's house" was a cottage dating to the time of Bob and Sissy's marriage, when they lived together there. Later, when Sissy moved to the converted barn, it was just Bob's house. During his periods at home he completed paintings and decorated pottery, a modest source of income.

Bob was a productive worker, but because he lived alone and was of reclusive habits, it was not known just how productively he used those twenty years. At his death the family entered the house and found tens of thousands of watercolors, drawings, and written journals (logs) amounting to four hundred thousand words. Viewed as a whole, they provide a natural history of the Gulf Coast in intimate detail.

When I got off that bus in Biloxi, the reverberations of a creative life resounded with no apparent diminishment twelve years after Bob's passing. That's what Mary was working on when I met her that June day. Technically speaking, she was organizing and cataloguing some of her father's ten thousand paintings and drawings. Emotionally, I would ultimately understand that these families clustered around Shearwater Pottery were themselves still discovering the Bob who was creatively and uniquely ablaze in those reclusive years.

Sissy and Mary quickly concluded I was a pilgrim. Who, after all, would ride a bus twenty hours and hike five miles with a backpack? Who would journey from western Arkansas to coastal Mississippi, with no knowledge at the time of what to expect? The wondering inside me must have been clear.

Sissy and her niece Patricia Findeisen—Peter and Patricia Anderson's daughter—were making a trip to Horn Island in January. Would I like to come?

For those with an itch for the sea, Horn Island is relatively close, even to Arkansas. It's a good place for provincial types like me to feel the sea.

You can get to Ocean Springs from Arkansas in a lot less than twenty hours in a decent car. For Sissy, Horn Island is right out the back door.

Sissy and her sister Patricia Grinstead were reared at Oldfields, a pecan plantation in Gautier next-door to Ocean Springs. From their porch they could see the lights from an old family home on Horn Island. In the days before air conditioning, coastal families sailed shallow draft catboats the few miles out to Horn and other barrier islands for picnics. The keel could be pulled up to allow the boat to maneuver in for beach landings. They spread blankets on Horn's east tip where sea breeze keeps mosquitoes at bay.

Sissy and Patricia married two Anderson boys, Bob and his older brother Peter. Patricia Anderson Findeisen was reared on the pottery grounds in the big house facing the Gulf. With the open sea almost off the front porch, the influence of the barrier islands was strong in her upbringing. As was the case with her mother and aunt, she made numerous trips with family and friends in a boat built by her father Peter.

Bob began solo journeys to Horn Island in World War II. Then in his forties, he took off in his small skiff from the marsh below the pottery. Powered by muscle and wind, his skiff allowed him to reach nature on terms suitable to his temperament and artistic interests. He worked his way east along the Gulf shore and, depending on wind and weather, pushed, rowed, towed, poled, or sailed. It wasn't that he couldn't have had a bigger, fancier boat. People sometimes offered him a tow, which he refused. Habit was intertwined with decided purpose. "One of the great mistakes of modern times," he wrote, "is to confuse eagles and aeroplanes."

There was a more specifically practical side to this habit, too. Horn is surrounded by shallow water. Nothing but a small boat can land directly on the beach. As a result, even though it's a only few miles from the mainland, it remains undeveloped. The folks who knew Horn best were fishermen and hunters. Horn was designated a National Wildlife Refuge in 1958, swept into the Gulf Islands National Seashore in 1971, and added to the national wilderness system in 1978. A modest ranger station was established, but otherwise it remains today much as Bob knew it—and as tropical storms continue to shape it.

Patricia Anderson (Findeisen) on Horn Island in January 1979. Like her Uncle Bob, Patricia enjoyed drawing, journaling, and studying nature while hiking around the island. She used her drawings and studies in pottery decorations for Shearwater Pottery.

Our midwinter visit is courtesy of Gulf Islands National Seashore. At the opening of 1979, I will share the island with an Anderson family friend, John Bryan. Sissy and her niece Patricia will be out for the second week.

The Park Service transports us in a thirty-six-foot boat with twin diesel engines. The pilot is skilled in the fine art of picking a path through the shallows immediately off Ocean Springs. Once in deeper water, he opens up the engines, leaving a great wake, and scattering Lesser Scaups, Redheads, and Common Loons. Horn seems to rise from the Gulf. At first we see only bare tips of pine trees.

Our big, convenient, fast boat can't run ashore, unlike the catboats of old and Bob's skiffs. Goods and people are loaded into a small boat. Being a true landlubber, I have no idea what to do with any kind of boat. John Bryan handles navigation chores.

Now we figure it's goodbye civilization, hello wilderness, or at least something like that. And in many respects—especially when compared to our normal routines—that's what happens. We are to "camp" in the ranger station where the accommodations—for those who aspire to some knowledge of wilderness—are blushingly adequate. Indeed, someone has advertised the "Horn Island Hilton" on the front door. House, shed, and water system are modern. Conveniences include hot water, gas stove, frig, central heat, and TV. We can call home on ship-to-shore radio (no cell phones in 1978). In return, we are responsible for some modest chores that require an hour; then we are ready for adventure. We have plenty of time to hike and as things turn out, bird watch.

For hikes Sissy pulls on black crabber's boots, heavy trousers, Navy pea coat, and a headscarf held in place by a white golfer's visor. Patricia wears her jeans stuck in green rubber boots, a yellow down ski jacket, and carries drawing materials in a small orange backpack. Sissy carries a stadium seat she can use for back support while sitting on the beach. Both women have binoculars for bird watching.

With Sissy in the lead, we head to the broad Gulf beach. A bamboo staff keeps her steady and provides a tool for probing objects washed up on the beach. "Dominant feature—sand white as snow," she writes in her journal. Then "The pine stands out singly—collectively, vertical trunks that rise to bursts of foliage . . . Shapes that have been twisted by wind and tide and strange earth pull."

Away from the beach and inside the island, she describes, "grass flats, salty, water-filled . . . lace-edged waves depositing their burdens of beauty . . ."

The trail from the Hilton comes out at a tidal pool typically attended by various combinations of gulls, terns, ducks, herons, and egrets. We have been on Horn Island just a couple of hours, but already the roar of twin diesels on the boat is marvelously replaced by Gulf surf. We walk east, along the high drift line, picking like curious raccoons through drift: pieces of boats, lumber, green bottles, light bulbs, fishing floats, hunks of multicolored rope, broken seashells, wine bottles, Budweiser cans. Animal tracks abound, both avian and mammalian. From a short distance we see some working birds: having pecked a round hole through its top, Fish Crows enjoy an orange.

From the tide line, we drift toward the dunes. Storm-twisted live oaks are dominant, with masses of waist-high rosemary bushes. There's also goldenrod, some with a few late blooms that hang on to the last warm days of fall. We gladly receive this island greeting. We walk among the low groves of palmetto whose swordlike leaves guard dunes.

The woods are marked by an irregular series of pines, reddened on

Sissy Anderson on the front steps of the "Horn Island Hilton" in January 1979. Volunteers were allowed to stay at the Hilton when Park Service rangers were away on other duties.

their seaward side by salt spray and hurricane twisted. The surf's roar is muffled in the pine barrens, well inside the dunes. It's easy to imagine that we are alone, in a wilderness, ears highly sensitive to all sounds. There are distant deep horns of cargo ships passing on Horn's east side into the Intercoastal Waterway. Suddenly comes the violent SWOOSH SWOOSH SWOOSH of a low-flying helicopter. Pine trees shake violently. The island seems to shake. The helicopter passes. We return to the beach and the comfort of pounding surf.

Sissy retires to her bed after supper, spiral notebook spread before her. "It is sheer bliss being here," she writes. "I went out to look at the glorious sunset, then to see these stars that can only be seen as intended, away from Man's myriad lights, and glowing . . ."

Sissy is busy the whole time, often with her journal. "Waking to unaccustomed brightness, we were up and out early," she writes. "I wanted to savor the predawn tenderness—the gentle suffusion, the blushings, prelude to the sun's love affair with the earth . . ." Sometimes she wears her Navy coat, sometimes her green Park Service jacket. This was a gift from son Johnny, who was a seasonal ranger after the park was established.

She takes her bamboo staff firmly in hand and strolls down the sandy trail to Rabbit Springs, Horn's chief source of fresh water. Spring is here, even in January. "Overhead the pines are blossoming," Sissy observes, and "underfoot the minuscules, tiny yellow stars, almost like miniature reflections of those above . . ." This walk was also Bob's daily ritual over his twenty years of trips here.

At Rabbit Springs, she lays down the bamboo staff, stoops to the well, drinks with cupped hands. "It makes me appreciate Ocean Springs' old role in the world of medicinal springs . . . Somehow this natural artesian flow tastes like health personified—sulphur and molasses—spring tonic." She goes there in rain and in freezing cold. Weary and sometimes painful bones do not deter. It takes a drink from Rabbit Springs to start her Horn Island day.

During the previous year Sissy had been to Horn with her daughter Mary, her niece Marge and assorted grandchildren. Here Sissy had celebrated the start of her seventieth year with a long hike. The plan was to circle the east point, fourteen miles total. Sissy stumbled on a log near the beginning. She insisted on continuing, adding a second staff and nursing a sore ankle. She rested more often than she had in past years. "The sand is compliant," she wrote. "It appears to accommodate the shape of my body, to the weight of my bones, their hardness. But, when I rise, it is my body that has stiffened to the quartz grains."

A year had passed and the ankle still hurt. An X-ray showed it broken and mended. Sissy was not deterred from hikes. "I'm up to them by virtue of desire," she states. She intends to enjoy Horn Island again, but she has another purpose, too. There had been an incessant demand that she produce a Walter Anderson biography.

The book is shaping up in morning walks to Rabbit Springs and under starry skies in evenings. Surf music and raucous Laughing Gulls sculpt her thoughts. She is busy with the task of, as she puts it, "Placing the man in his place and time." Of course, Bob had been alone most of

The open sky above lovely Horn Island. With its white sand, native shrubs and grasses, and scattered mature pines, Horn is a wilderness, changeless in some respects, but as Walter Anderson noted, rearranged by every storm from the Gulf of Mexico.

those Horn Island years, so Sissy has a research project on her hands. Patricia, John Bryan, and I are immediate beneficiaries. She shares a sort of island roadmap with us: his island crossing paths; favorite camping spots; pools where he bathed or stalked birds, pencil and paper in hand; and the best places to find alligators. We hear tales about the young Bob and the older Horn Island wanderer—all this and a good supper in the Hilton.

Giving mental shape to a book is only part of it, maybe the superficial part. Sissy is in deep wonder at her own life, how it became enmeshed in Bob's, about how this skinny sliver of sand—so much part of their lives—seems to change with every tide. The big hurricanes tear Horn to pieces. And yet, in many respects, Horn seems virtually unchanged from her childhood. It must be a kind of alchemy, this dance between wind, sand, and sea.

"The lonely one who lodged here is much with me," she writes. "He, who found solace in his own soul and in Nature's matter-of-fact presence and beauty, a beauty he could help into expression by painting it again and again—color, pattern of this island."

She does not directly say these things to me, a virtual stranger. But casual supper talk suggests the purposes of her daytime wanderings.

Like Sissy, Patricia is up early, often before daylight. She skips breakfast in order to get out at the earliest hour. Her goal is the beach trail where she counts animal tracks, one of our responsibilities. Like Bob's logs and drawings, the tracks are a valuable addition to the island's natural history. It's a busy place of cottontails, mice, birds, hogs, and frogs. Occasionally, snakes or alligators leave messages. Paws and a round tail dragged in unbroken line are evidence of nutria. No water margin is complete without its five-toed coon tracks.

After identifying the tracks, Patricia often hikes west from the Hilton through sandy pine savannahs of palmetto and rosemary toward freshwater marshes. Here even in the supposed dead of winter, Horn Island is decked in gay attire. The palmettos are busy unfolding deep green fans. Delicate, needle-like rosemary leaves sport lemon-yellow berries. The pine's future is obvious in the purple buds within an inviting cone whirl. Down toward the marsh, fluffy silvery heads atop russet stalks mark beardgrass.

Like her uncle Bob, Patricia draws on typewriter paper. Her quick pen-and-ink line drawings emphasize basic forms and essential movements. The pines are a few vertical lines broken by squared suggestions of bark. Branches are curved horizontals decorated with short feathery lines of needles. Seeing three Great Egrets overhead, she presents their broad wings and curved necks in a harmony of movement.

Gray-blue berries of midwinter cover stout myrtle shrubs. Red berries decorate yaupon shrubs. Visiting both are flocks of warblers constantly giving *check-check* calls and flashing distinctive bright yellow rump patches—Yellow-rumped Warblers. Shrubs give way to a thick carpet of spike rush, saw grass, slash pine—all braided together with greenbrier, just then festooned by clusters of shiny black berries. On Patricia's drawing pad this becomes curling heart-shaped leaves with butterflies attending masses of black berries.

Upon reaching the water, Patricia finds a hiding place. She observes the black-feathered, ivory-billed American Coots, and their cousins, the

Big dead pine snag atop a dune on Horn Island. It had seen many a powerful storm, yet thrived. *Drawing in the field by Joe Neal in January 1979.*

red-billed, greenish-legged Common Gallinules. Gallinules pump their heads with each foot stroke. They fly reluctantly. Alarmed, they swim silently among cattails. As Patricia sits quietly, they slowly emerge from among cattails.

Her drawings record a Great Blue Heron's upright watchfulness in shallow water. Slight wave action is suggested by a few curls as the bird slowly wades away.

Horn Island is my first real birding adventure. Patricia sometimes uses binoculars to spot birds for her drawing. Sissy, who is losing her eyesight, says she doesn't need hers. The fascination with birds seen through binoculars takes hold of me. I begin surveying the world through Sissy's binoculars.

From the Horn Hilton, it's approximately seven miles east or west to the points where sand turns to sea. Three miles east is a cluster of high dunes topped by half-buried oaks and piles of much weathered red bricks that mark the home of the Waters family, island farmers from 1845 to 1920. It was lights from the Waters's place that Sissy could see as a girl. On the Gulf beach beyond is the wasting hulk of the shrimp trawler *Arcturus,* blown aground in a storm, and abandoned—and a great perch for gulls and terns.

I spend a long rainy day wandering with Sissy's binoculars and trying to look up birds in my Peterson Field Guide without getting everything soaked. A yellowthroat peers at me through cattails, all black mask and bright yellow. A catbird mews from yaupons. At one point I wade through a marsh but don't get far. I identify the Rusty Blackbirds and Red-winged Blackbirds, and then the Boat-tailed Grackles. Rusties blend wonderfully with the yellows and browns of marsh grasses.

Back on the beach, I saw thousands of ducks offshore. Trying to identify them, I flip desperately between binoculars and Peterson: binos—book, binos—book, binos—book, until my eyes are burning. It is like that all day, between the beach and the island ponds. I identify Buffleheads, Redheads, Canvasbacks, one of the scaup species, probably Surf Scoter, certainly some big, green-headed Mallards, and what seems a Red-breasted Merganser.

Four miles west from the Hilton is a brackish marsh dominated by black rushes. Clapper Rails are common along the edge. Beyond is an inlet on the north Mississippi Sound beach that flows with the tides. The lagoon is a magnet for fishermen, Great Egrets, Tricolored Herons, and Little Blue Herons. Shorebirds like Black-bellied Plovers and several gull species gather at the point of sand facing the Mississippi Sound. Common Loons are numerous in the sound. Ospreys plunge for fish, talons-first, above the lagoon. Their bulky nests are visible in the dead upper limbs of mature pines.

Patricia and I bird together. She shows me her special gallinule pond, a family-sized place, resplendent in cattails and cold blue water. There are three gallinules and two coots. We spot what I believed is a Peregrine Falcon in a big pine.

I am thoroughly soaked after days of birding in rain and marshes. The Peterson guide is waterlogged and thereafter essentially useless. Unfortunately, it is basically the same for Sissy's binoculars. Sissy is gracious. In future years I will afford higher-priced waterproof and fog-proof binoculars, but none have will deliver more exciting and valuable service than Sissy's on a Horn Island winter day, now many years ago.

Sadly, it's February 1. Our time is ending. The morning has been cool, but it's seventy by noon. I have slipped out of my January long johns

Walter Anderson celebrated all the wild creatures of Horn Island, including long-legged waders like the Great Egret and Snowy Egrets shown here.

and gone down to a T-shirt. I could wind up with some kind of stylish winter sunburn to take home to Arkansas.

From a distance the marsh seems so calm, so much like an endless Ozark meadow. I walk several miles, skirting marsh and pools. I hear the *kuk-kuk-kuk-kuk* of coots or maybe *klack klack klack* of Clapper Rails? Or maybe neither, but interesting. Quietly as possible I peer through leaf and stem, wanting the completely undisturbed view. There are the coots, fine-looking Redheads, Pied-billed Grebes, gallinules, plus the two big wading birds—Great Blue Heron and Great Egret. Flocks of metallic blue-green Tree Swallows pour through and among the pines and shrubs, snapping up insects. Purple Martins plunge to the water's surface with such vigor and in such numbers that the grebes sometimes dive to avoid them.

The air smells of salt and sulphur. High overhead I see a hawk whose brilliant tail illuminates reddish like cathedral glass. I walk on toward the big lagoon and there see a raccoon using all four feet to probe the sandy bottom. I crouch down in the black rushes and watch

Least Terns nest on beaches and dive for fish in shallow waters along the shoreline. Wilderness areas like Horn Island are especially important to them because beachfront development and increasing recreational use has greatly reduced their suitable nesting habitat.

the coon scoop up a crab, which is promptly munched down like a hamburger, legs flailing to the end.

Now it's time to turn back toward the Hilton and meet our boat. I'm collecting a few souvenirs along the tide—cockles, coquinas, and empty horseshoe crab shells. Here are the raccoon's tracks, plus those of hog and heron. I take off my boots and leave a few tracks of my own.

John Bryan has been checking the Hilton's generator and then joins Patricia and Sissy for a quick visit to Bob's old camp. I find their tracks near the Hilton: three pairs of boots and the round point of Sissy's staff where it poked along the tide. They're silent when I catch up with them.

Good surf has come up, roaring the beaches. The south wind is catching the crest, holding it briefly as a spray, then blowing it back, undulating rainbows across the sunset. "You miss things without realizing what you are missing," Bob wrote, "then blame yourself for insensitivity—the truth is that things move fast, and life is interesting and there are many things to be enjoyed and digested . . ."

Chronologically speaking, it's now many years ago that I visited Horn Island. On my bookshelf in Fayetteville I have Sissy's 1989 memoir, *Approaching the Magic Hour: Memories of Walter Anderson*. The following passage recounts Sissy's feelings in 1966, a year after Bob passed. She was on a family trip to Horn Island.

> I walked the beach and came to that remnant of the dune where he had camped. . . . Climbing the slant, which was covered in the browned needles of a small dead pine, I felt such sorrow, such yearning that I slid down against the narrow trunk. For a time I sat, a blank sorrow gripping me . . . After a while I became aware of a shining, and looking down the slope I saw a lily pond sparkling full in the sun. Suddenly I felt his presence, this man of light . . . I was with him . . .
>
> A flight of redwings slid across the space. They lit close. These were his friends, returned from winter travels. The three notes they sang over and over were the song they had shared with him. The terrible sense of loss dissipated . . . I felt him close as I walked down the beach. . . .

A tropical storm in 1906 blew away the old Horn Island light, plus the keeper. Storms in 1916 and 1947 damaged the island. Hurricane Betsy in 1965 washed away Bob's favorite campsite that Sissy had visited. Of Betsy, Bob wrote, "Never has there been a more respectable hurricane . . . The awful sunrise—no one could fail to take warning from it—the hovering black spirit bird, the man of war, just one, comme il faut."

A storm in 1969 took half a mile off the east end of the island and deposited enough fresh sand on the west end to almost make up the loss. Hurricane Frederick in 1979 damaged Horn's pine forest and washed away more of the east point.

And so it goes, to Katrina, in 2005.

The Katrina that flooded New Orleans killed 1,300 and made homeless 250,000 people. It washed over Horn, Shearwater Pottery, plus most of Ocean Springs and Biloxi. The bridge I walked over in 1977 was smashed. The pottery as I knew it from the late 1970s is now a memory. Nine family homes were lost, plus six other buildings. Walter Anderson's house and the pottery workshop sustained heavy damage. Sissy's barn and the old house where Patricia grew up were also victims.

The main evidence of Katrina in Arkansas was a rash of rare bird sightings. Whole flocks of Laughing Gulls were blown up from the Gulf; they are a great rarity here so far inland. Arkansas had several Magnificent Frigatebirds, Bob's man-of-wars, the hovering black spirits —also a great rarity inland. "Comme il faut" as he wrote: a proper result of a proper and violently destructive hurricane.

Broken pottery and other artwork littered the ruins of Shearwater Pottery in Katrina's wake. A vault with many of the family's personal collections of Bob's work was flooded. None of the Andersons or related families living in Ocean Springs were among the 1300 dead in New Orleans and along the coast. The Walter Anderson Museum of Art in Ocean Springs suffered only modest damage.

Katrina flattened Shearwater's buildings, but not its spirit. In an interview broadcast on National Public Radio, Mary recounted her father's love of storms. She noted the presence of new beginnings: birds have returned to the denuded landscape. The process of salvaging what could be salvaged got under way immediately.

In 2010, five years after Katrina, British Petroleum's Deepwater Horizon well exploded and sank in the Gulf, producing one of the greatest spills of crude oil the world has seen. It spread oil all over Walter Anderson's world.

I have a very cool little art book of drawings called *Pelicans*. Line drawings of Brown Pelicans by Walter Anderson are at the book's core. The story of her father's art and these particular drawings are presented by Mary Anderson Pickard, whom I met so long ago in Ocean Springs. The book is about mangroves, Brown Pelicans, frigatebirds, fiddler crabs in mangroves, and one man's celebration.

Mary writes, "In the late 1940s and 50s, Anderson reveled in the 'tremendously musical harmonies' of thousands of nesting pelicans in the Chandeleur rookeries on North Key . . ." The Chandeleur Islands, part of Breton National Wildlife Refuge—that's a place where a lot of the oil went ashore, oiling eggs and nestlings, with adult Brown Pelicans diving in oiled water.

A few years after making these drawings, Walter Anderson began to notice the decline in nesting Brown Pelicans. No one then understood

Brown Pelicans and Laughing Gulls provided inspiration for the art of Walter Anderson. They are still familiar sights along the Gulf Coast and inspire our better natures, too.

DDT. Anderson passed away in 1965, a few years after the publication of the alarm bell *Silent Spring* by Rachel Carson. He did not live to see the bitter fight over banning DDT and the subsequent slow return of pelicans to the Gulf. Nor did he live to see the pelicans return so strongly that they were removed from the list of endangered species in 2009.

Anderson was onto something in honoring "tremendously musical harmonies." It seems a useful goal as these agonies play out and we try to figure out where as a society we go from here, post–Deepwater Horizon. His drawings remain. They remind us in a timely fashion.

Doug James (with binoculars) and Bill Beall at Ponca, in the valley of the Buffalo River, April 2007. They began their friendship more than fifty years ago with birding adventures at Lake Fayetteville when Doug was a young professor in zoology and Bill a business undergraduate.

Cave Mountain

AN INDIGO BUNTING'S bright singing hangs above the Buffalo. Looking up, I see where a bluff line intertwines with fluffy clouds. It's June 1979 in Newton County. Doug James and I have hiked a big loop from where Steel Creek flows into the Buffalo River. American Redstarts sing from cool shadows. We've settled on an island with a broad beach formed by smooth cobbles and sand. Dominating the pool is a ship-size sandstone monarch tumbled down from the bluff above. A Louisiana Waterthrush *chip*s from the edge of a noisy riffle and flies up the creek.

The monarch rock broke free from its mooring on the bluff above ages ago. Canoeists attempt to dodge it during their spring floats. They don't all make the dodge, as evidenced by red, blue, and green plastic scrapes. A native throne, it invites turtles and summer loungers; it's a convenient place for us to haul out from the river. Hogsuckers and smallmouth bass swim in the clear water below its protective overhang, part form, part shadow.

This was in 1979.

Doug relaxes on a plastic raft. For a few hours he lounges far from an extraordinarily busy schedule with his students, who that summer are involved in an ecological study of the upper Buffalo River funded by the National Science Foundation—birds, plants, Native American sites, small mammals. They are looking broadly at the Buffalo valley ecosystem. The Buffalo had become America's first National River after a long and ultimately successful fight to stop construction of two dams.

The bunting sings bright doublets from a cottonwood limb overhanging the pool, partially shading our big rock. I see its brilliant blue against cottonwood green and the smooth brown-gray bluff rising to storm twisted cedars and shortleaf pines. The Buffalo and its shadows keep real summer heat at bay.

I met Doug in 1977 in what today is named the Anne Kittrell Art Gallery on the University of Arkansas–Fayetteville campus. I was recently returned from a trip to the Mississippi Gulf Coast. Initially I'd gone there out of curiosity about Walter Inglis Anderson, naturalist painter. Anderson died in 1965, but I met his family and with them made a trip to Horn Island where he had painted many of his watercolor masterpieces. The Andersons offered to loan some of his paintings for a show on the University of Arkansas campus. Many paintings involved birds. Doug identified them and helped prepare notes for the exhibit. Working with him on the birds became the first of what would be many field trips over several decades.

Gifted with sensitive ears and sharp eyes, Doug could have been a Native American hunter, a scout in the old West, artist of first rank. He chose birds or, perhaps, birds chose him. That is, maybe the birds anointed him with their varied forms and exquisite songs. Birds certainly infected him with their charismatic enthusiasm for life.

He was born in Detroit in 1925 and began leading field trips as a boy. That would be at age eight, when he was in the third grade. It was a mile of woods and fields between his home and grade school. He learned the plants first and his third-grade teacher got him to lead field trips. Other teachers also discovered his talents, and he went back to the grade school to lead field trips through his junior-high years. On one of these trips he heard a goldfinch behind a fencerow. He told the students that if they could be quiet and just creep behind him, he could show them the bird. There was amazement all around when the goldfinch was seen. How could he do it? Just by ears alone? Now as a senior scientist, he leads undergraduate and graduate students in discovery of Arkansas's avian gold. In between, there's been a lot of birding and travel.

Take for example his military service in the 1950s. Since he joined the zoology faculty at U of A in 1953, he served required years as a research associate in the U.S. Army Chemical Corps at Pine Bluff Arsenal, Arkansas. This facility is devoted to something average people can't stand to think about, or even imagine, but which militaries and powerful politicians worldwide just can't get enough of: weapons of mass destruction. The arsenal is devoted to germ-warfare research and development. Doug's job—no surprise here—mainly birds. When asked about his service, he says he helped make germ-warfare bombs.

Our lazy talk along the Buffalo turns to a trip he took to the Philippines. This was during those dark ages before one could obtain a bird book for virtually any place in the world simply with a call to the American Birding Association, or Buteo Books—and years before Amazon.com and the global ebook store. He relied on the old-fashioned method of writing observations with a lead pencil in a notebook. There was scrupulous attention to how the bird looked, behaved, vocalized—the bird's jizz (a British acronym for "general impression of size and shape") and specific habitat notations.

Returning to the United States, he stopped off at the bird skin collection in the Smithsonian Institution. He was able to identify most of the Philippine birds with his field notes, plus memory. But then there are those few . . . He described these to Storrs Olson, curator of birds, who rattled off appropriate Latin binomials. These were added to his trip notes.

Doug has taught the value of writing observations to a half-century's worth of ornithology students. A short lead pencil and a flexible surveyor's notebook with bright yellow cover are still required in his course. It's about the same way Thomas Nuttall took notes during his trip through Arkansas Territory in 1819. It worked then and it works now, even in the age of ever more sophisticated electronic note-taking gadgets.

We are briefly recalled from Doug's Philippine reverie to the Buffalo River by constant bunting songs and less frequent calls from a Yellow-billed Cuckoo. Old settlers knew it as the "rain crow" because its *coo coo coo cow cow cow* song predicted showers. It sounds up the river from us, in a little thicket of willow saplings.

Doug associates this with another hot summer when he was in India. There he became familiar with the Common Hawk Cuckoo, locally called the "brain fever bird." According to Doug, in the afternoon when it is deadly hot and everyone is sensibly napping, this cuckoo loudly sings *brain fever, Brain Fever, BRAIN FEVER*. Doug's voice sounds strange because his nose is a little plugged from the cool Buffalo water and also, yes, because of his cuckoo rendition.

We watch water snakes weaving silently among limbs and leaves piled up against the big rock. Doug recalls graduate-student days at the University of Michigan in the late 1940s. He was birding in swampland, wearing tennis shoes. Then as now, his field shoes were his oldest running shoes. There's a constant tapping on one foot. He barely notices because an interesting bird flits from leaf to leaf high above, and Doug has his head craned way up in his eagerness to give it a name. After he cinches the female Blackburnian Warbler, he looks down upon a constantly striking Massasauga rattler.

Five decades of Jamesian ornithological pursuits means tens of thousands of field hours. Unlike the typical Massasauga, not all rattlers encountered are small. Once he caught a big one and hiked two miles with it to a gas station. Men who saw him coming escaped via the back door. They saw, not the biologist with his prized specimen, but rather an attacking lunatic. "Could have held the place up," Doug summarizes.

Less dangerously, Doug is fond of demystifying tarantulas. He takes his ecology students high on a hill above the Buffalo River and finds some that have lived for years in an old rock pile. Tentatively, they walk on his outstretched hand, and up his arm. Students are fascinated. They've never met such a person. Most hold back. But tentatively, one and then another reaches out to touch the big spider.

He didn't know about ornithology as a third grader. Later, he assumed he would have to teach high school biology if he was going to be an ornithologist. He took education courses as an undergraduate at the University of Michigan with that career in mind. He found that typical education courses didn't suit his interests. Then he met a professor and researcher who was an ornithologist. Thereafter, the path forward was clear.

A Kentucky Warbler sings from a moist thicket in the island loop behind us. Turkey Vultures soar over the bluff and down the Buffalo Valley.

Several years after that Buffalo afternoon, Doug and I are out in river bottom woods near Fayetteville. Our quarry includes high pitched *zee zeet zee zeet* calls of Blue-gray Gnatcatchers and equally high ones of Black-and-white Warblers. Birders describe this warbler's song as a "squeaky wheel that needs oiling."

At sixty, Doug can't run as fast as in his youth—that's OK, he can make adjustments, and just slow down. But it seems his trusty ears are also yielding to age—a big problem, since he still has many students and he has no intention to slow down teaching and birding. It is well known that as men age they tend to lose the higher range in their hearing at a rate somewhat faster than women. It may be that men more often fire guns, run chainsaws, and operate drills. Maybe it's why women often seem better listeners. Or maybe it's hardwired into genes.

Doug has decided to experiment. That's where I come in—a younger man by two decades, ears probably closer than his to 100 percent, at least, at the higher pitches. This is a test. Can Doug hear gnatcatchers when they are close? Can he hear them at ten yards? We compare ears.

Turns out, I hear them. He can't, unless close.

For birders, ears are akin to a mechanic's tools. This is true in Doug's case especially, since he is the "Father" of the Breeding Bird Survey in Arkansas. The BBS is a bird counting research effort 90 percent dependent upon participants' ability to accurately hear bird calls at distances up to one-fourth mile away. Blue-gray Gnatcatchers and Black-and-white Warblers are two common nesting birds in western Arkansas. We wonder what else he can't hear.

BBS routes are set up all over the country. Each route has fifty equal stops along 24.5 miles. The surveyor counts all birds seen and heard for three minutes each one-half mile. Routes are run every June. It's possible to see trends in such a mass of data. Populations of some birds like Red-eyed Vireos increase. Some like Blue-gray Gnatcatcher seem to remain stable. Cerulean Warblers decline.

Why do some increase and others decline? What's happening in the environment to stimulate observed changes? With his hearing loss, Doug knows he can no longer effectively participate in this survey.

Compton BBS covers the Buffalo River country in Newton County. It begins at 5:34 a.m. in grassy upland pastures and former prairies of the Ozarks on Arkansas 43 near the junction of the Carroll, Boone, and Newton County lines. Open pastures and post oaks surround Stop 1. Small farms are scattered along the highway. There are Eastern Meadowlarks and Blue Grosbeaks in the fields. Chipping Sparrows call from open woodlands. Chuck-will's-widows sing in the predawn darkness. A Great Horned Owl may perch in a snag near Stop 1.

Give or take a few minutes, Stop 1 is ninety minutes from Fayetteville. It means rising at 3:30 a.m. Doug and his graduate students have performed most of the Compton surveys. More recently, Compton

Forested Ozark hills above early morning fog in Buffalo River Valley can be seen from several spots in the highlands of the Compton Breeding Bird Survey route, northern Newton County, June 2003.

is the birding bailiwick of a friend who can still hear the numerous gnatcatchers along this route, and many species of warblers, including Black-and-whites. In other words, I've inherited Compton.

As a crow flies, Stop 1 is about six miles north of our swimming hole. The route ends at Stop 50 on Cave Mountain, about eleven miles south, also as a crow flies. By the way, it could be either American Crow or Fish Crow.

The first eight miles or sixteen stops are generally in the uplands at an elevation of 2100 to 2300 feet, more than 1000 feet above the Buffalo River. This is the old Ozark Plateau tableland with hayfields and pastures. Compton is a crossroads with a country store.

There are small homes old and new, pastures and hayfields large and small, and patches of forest along these miles. Most of the country has been converted from native prairies to cool-season grasses like fescue. Many folks who live here farm part-time and also work in towns like Harrison.

One of the bigger hayfields sometimes hosts Grasshopper Sparrows

(Stop 5). Orchard Orioles sing in small woodlots around farmhouses. Bobwhites are common around small farms. The most numerous birds here are Indigo Buntings. An extensive field at Stop 13 is unique with its big bluestem and other native grasses and shrubs. It hosts Blue-winged and Prairie Warblers.

After Stop 16, Compton BBS descends one thousand feet into the valley of the Buffalo. It requires about two miles along Arkansas 43 to drop into Ponca village. Along the way is a forested bluff line with views of wide valleys to the west through which flow Buffalo tributaries. With its complex plant communities, this rough country is attractive to a host of Neotropical songbirds.

I frequently find Ovenbirds, Kentucky Warblers, Acadian Flycatchers, and Scarlet Tanagers. The valley overlook along Highway 43 has my ears alert for Wood Thrushes. I look out over the forest canopy for soaring Broad-winged Hawks. Some of the commonest birds here are Red-eyed Vireos. They prefer mature forest with a dense mid-story of small trees. I can hear three or four from one spot.

Stop 18 overlooks the green Buffalo Valley. In the early light there may be a dense gray fog filling the valley like an ocean. Green hills crisscross and seem to float through the sky like some truly vast Renaissance painting. Stop 22 invariably yields a singing Louisiana Waterthrush along Ponca Creek. Several Ponca stops provide me the opportunity to hear a Wood Thrush dawn chorus from forested slopes. American Redstarts call among understory trees.

Just beyond Stop 24 is an 1850 log house built by William Villines for his bride Rebecca. This is near the Buffalo River highway bridge at the intersection of Highways 43 and 74. Elk frequent the highway in this area. A phoebe sings from a log outbuilding. I wonder how passage of 150 years has changed what William and Rebecca heard in their time?

The BBS courses eight miles, more or less, through the Buffalo valley, sometimes in view of the river, and sometimes in view of elk grazing in bottomland fields. I hear Pileated Woodpeckers drumming on distant unseen snags. Red-winged Blackbirds call in hayfields. Barn Swallows sweep over farms and perch on wires. Blue-gray Gnatcatchers escort their young, already out of the nest.

Adult Wood Duck males and females parade with their broods of ducklings at Stop 32 alongside Boxley millpond. Usually I find a

Wood Ducks nest in forests along the Buffalo National River, and flocks including adults and young are common on the old millpond at Boxley, as seen in this photograph on September 13, 2010.

Yellow Warbler singing in the tall sycamores on the pond's east side and Common Yellowthroats in buttonbush thickets. It's difficult to keep this stop to three minutes, but three minutes is all that is allowed.

At Stop 34 I get my first glimpse of majestic Cave Mountain, towering in the south above the Boxley church. Stop 36 is at the foot of Cave Mountain. Hooded Warblers and Northern Parulas sing in the riparian forest. From an elevation of 1100 feet, the route climbs precipitously toward 2100–2200 feet in just over a mile, ascending the northeastern slope of Cave Mountain. The forest here is cooler and generally retains more moisture. This in turn fosters a rich understory of pawpaws and umbrella magnolias. Beech trees are common. Ovenbirds nest on the forest floor.

About halfway up is a small parking area for Bat Cave, with hibernating colonies of rare Gray Bats and Indiana Bats. An Eastern Phoebe nests in the cave's entrance and Yellow-throated Vireos sing from mature trees. The gravel road hangs from the mountainside. Big trees and huge chunks of the bluff line from above have fallen down slope.

Gifts of this daunting mountain road include grand views of

birds typically at neck-straining heights in the canopy—like Cerulean Warblers. Because trees are rooted on the slopes below, birds almost impossible to see elsewhere are easy pickings in canopies nearly at eye level. Massive green canopies of mature beeches, red oaks, and shagbark hickories present themselves at a convenient height vis-à-vis an observer on Cave Mountain Road.

Worm-eating Warblers chip from among the massive boulders with tangles of grape and poison ivy. There is a whole mountainside of Wood Thrushes singing from the pawpaw thickets below and extending all the way to the Buffalo. There is a great spot to get out of the car and sit on a huge broken piece of the bluff and just listen. It will just wring the urban fatigue right out of your soul to sit for that Wood Thrush concert. But remember—only for three minutes—then on to the next stop. I can return, but only after Stop 50 is recorded on the data sheets.

The Cave Mountain ascent is accomplished at an elevation of 2150 feet. Stop 39 is at the top. The Upper Buffalo Wilderness and Ozark National Forest dominate the remaining miles. Generally this is a dry forest. Mainly I hear Eastern Wood-Pewees, Ovenbirds, Summer Tanagers, Black-and-white Warblers, and White-breasted Nuthatches, plus scattered Wood Thrushes. There are a few farms along the road and bluebirds in open hilltop pastures. I sometimes find Eastern Towhees in thickets around abandoned farm places.

Stop 48 is near a small parking area used by visitors to Hawksbill Crag, in the Upper Buffalo Wilderness. The Forest Service has erected a carved boulder here. It reads, "Special thanks to Senator Dale Bumpers for his outstanding contribution to wilderness in Arkansas." Amen to that.

Stop 50, the end of the route, is near a small farm with cows, a few horses, and chickens in the yard. If this year is like most, it will be nearly 10:30 a.m. and the breeze will be coming up from the valley, stirring the deep green oak leaves. If I'm lucky, I hear the high-pitched *pweeee* of a soaring Broad-winged Hawk.

Now, close the book on this year's BBS and head back for the Wood Thrush concert. Thanks for passing it on, Doug.

Cave Mountain Road junctions with hardtop Highway 16 near Red Star. The highway then loops over the mountains in a westerly direction through the communities of Boston and Pettigrew. It continues through the valley of the White River from St. Paul into Fayetteville eventually. A lot of history has crossed the mountains.

Cave Mountain Road dates back at least to pioneer times. It got a big workout during the logging boom. A railroad, the St. Paul branch of the Fayetteville and Little Rock Railroad, was built from Fayetteville into this region starting in the mid-1880s. Branches were soon built in all directions, providing shipping to national markets. Many huge hardwood timbers were required for bridge construction. Millions of hardwood ties—eight feet long with sides six by eight inches —were required for the tracks here and in the western United States. Big white-oak forests were cut, primarily for the barrel-making industry. People in the mountains found an opportunity to work for cash, cutting this forest.

The Fayetteville Wagon-Wood and Lumber Company was organized in 1893. Drawing upon white oak, ash, and hickory timbers, the company manufactured carriage and wagon-wood stock, plow parts, and spokes. The Ozark Wagon Works, organized in 1897, turned out Ozark Wagons, advertised as "the finest on wheels."

These businesses sprung up as a direct result of the railroad construction that made it possible to efficiently ship heavy timbers. By 1887, the St. Paul branch was built east from Fayetteville into the hardwood forests. In 1897 the branch was extended another twelve miles to Pettigrew. The town trumpeted itself as "The Hardwood Capital of the World."

During the years 1903–1909, there was a boom in cutting virgin cedar forests in Newton County. It was impractical to haul logs over Cave Mountain to the Pettigrew railhead. Instead, logs were floated down the Buffalo River. At one time, 175,000 cedar logs were pushed into the river at Boxley and floated to a plant near Gilbert. Much of this wood was purchased by the Eagle Pencil Company, which sold their product for ten cents per dozen.

The logging boom went into decline, naturally enough, as the virgin hardwood was cut. But Cave Mountain Road had yet another role to play. The outbreak of World War I in 1914 created demand for minerals like zinc—for galvanizing iron, paint pigment, and battery electrodes—and for lead, which of course was the weapon of mass destruction in that time.

Zinc had been mined at Ponca as early as 1882, with lead ores in the same works. The ore was hauled twenty-five miles over rough Cave Mountain wagon road to the railhead at Pettigrew. The round trip required three days.

The timber business played out when forests were stripped of the best timber. The zinc-lead business played out with the end of the mass killing called World War I.

In 1908, President Theodore Roosevelt set aside over 900,000 acres that had been part of the federally controlled public domain in Arkansas. This became the core of the modern Ozark National Forest. It was the first such hardwood forest protected and eventually reclaimed in the country. Ecological recovery of the upper Buffalo River country is a direct result of Roosevelt's understanding of the need for public lands.

Now roll the clock forward to 1995, soon after I take over the Compton BBS from Doug. At ten years, my daughter Ariel is too old by years to go "birding" with me like we did when she was two. Of course, she no longer fits in the old backpack that worked so well when she was a baby. She is now too wise to overly interest herself in adult stuff, like the Compton BBS. However, she does still enjoying hanging around with Dad, especially in the summer, and especially when there is a chance to go to the Buffalo.

It occurs to me that those two words "Buffalo" and "River" are magical, conjuring fun just ahead. This is how I, crafty mature adult, bait her and her best friend Shawna, into this year's Compton BBS. They aren't deterred by the 3:30 a.m. rising. They willingly sleep in their bathing suits. I carry them out to my Chevy S-10 pickup, and dump them in the seat, belt 'em in. Our gear for the day—extra clothes, water, toys—is stuffed in two truck boxes.

Ariel and Shawna aren't awake for the Great Horned Owls at Stop 1, at 5:25. They aren't awake for Stop 13's Blue-winged Warblers. But they are kind of awake at Ponca, at 7:30. I suspect it's not the Wood Thrushes singing from the hillside that awakens them. It may be something primordial, like the magical earthy smell nearby of a big mountain river and its humid forest.

It's a little crowded in the S-10, especially as they become awake and start playing. Seat belts aren't very forgiving for energetic,

The clear and cool waters of the upper Buffalo River, with its gravel bars, sandstone bluffs and light early morning fog, invite us to stay a while. June 2006.

just-awake children. They aren't sensitive to the rigid standards of the BBS—three minutes per stop—half-mile drive—three-minute stop—no delays allowed. There's a brief necessary pee stop in the bushes near Stop 40. There's giggling, I tell them to hurry, and they return with a bright idea: how 'bout riding in the back of the pick up for the rest of the BBS?

I laugh and listen to Cerulean Warblers. Is that a Prothonotary down at the base of the mountain slope, at the river? Then I listen to muted sounds of two kids enjoying a special day in Newton County.

The route is done: 10:25 a.m. We head now for the Promised Land, where there will be more "stops," but these will be for snacks at the Ponca store and a finale at America's Finest Jumping Off Into A Natural, Free-Flowing River. That is, our final stop is at the Ponca low-water bridge over the Buffalo.

It's 11 a.m. on a June day deep in the forests of western Arkansas. The sun is shining and the air is warm. Dog-day cicadas are singing. A time-honored toe test indicates the water is "jest" right. That means it's as cold as ever. Daring each other to be the first to jump, they compromise, join hands, and jump feet first together. Their screams meld with the songs of a Yellow-throated Warbler in the sweet gum by the low water bridge, sap aromatic in the summer sunshine.

Needless to say, as the year 2007 rolls around, Ariel, Shawna, and other swim mates from those days no longer fit in the old S10. The little girls are all twenty-somethings. They love the Buffalo, but now they tend to go there in their own cars, with their own friends, and for their own purposes, just as Doug and I have done.

What happened along the Buffalo several decades ago is probably no better known to the average Buffalo National River visitor today than it is to the American Redstarts singing from shady thickets on the banks. Two large dams were once planned for the river's middle and lower sections. Resulting impoundments would have drowned significant sections of the river.

A big old silver aluminum canoe out in Doug James's Fayetteville backyard tells part of the story. It's constructed of extra-heavy aluminum. It will take a lot of rock bashing. It's a battleship compared to contemporary, multicolored canoes made from various light-weight ABS polymers. It dates to the 1950s, a relic of Doug's long affair with the Buffalo River.

I got to thinking about that Ouachita canoe while reading Neil Compton's *The Battle for the Buffalo River, A Twentieth-Century Conservation Crisis in the Ozarks* (University of Arkansas Press, 1992). Doug makes quite a bit more than a cameo appearance in this book. This battle was underway before I knew Doug, when I was in junior high and Doug was a new college professor. There's some insight into the man and his times.

The dam ideas date back to the 1940s, when plans were drawn to curb flooding in the vast watershed of the White River and its many tributaries, including the Buffalo. Most rivers in the watershed were dammed, but the Buffalo eventually escaped. Neil Compton's book tells the story. Many were involved in the effort to stop the dams, including Doug James.

This particular aspect of the battle for the Buffalo story dates to May 1955, when Doug, his former spouse Fran, and other birders founded the Arkansas Audubon Society. Besides being a founder, Doug served as corresponding secretary for its conservation committee. In this capacity, he sent letters to the Arkansas congressional delegation in opposition to the dams. The year was 1957. At that time, Arkansas Audubon Society and the Federated Garden Clubs of Arkansas stood basically alone in providing a statewide private citizen opposition to the dams and for a free-flowing river.

Just as he was a key player in founding the Arkansas Audubon Society, Doug was a founder of the Ozark Society, organized in 1962 specifically to stop the dams. In his capacity as a scientist, Doug led hikes in the Buffalo River country as dam opponents studied the region's unique ecology. He testified for a free-flowing river at public hearings (1962), and organized a student chapter of the Ozark Society at the University of Arkansas–Fayetteville (1964), involving students in the conservation fight. Doug hosted a Fayetteville meeting of the American Ornithologists' Union (1969) and took the AOU, including the famous artist Roger Tory Peterson, for a firsthand look at the Buffalo.

Many people were involved in this fight, which reached an end stage in 1972 with the creation of the Buffalo National River. But, of course, the fight at the core of the Buffalo River controversy is never over. Here's what Neil Compton had to say about this in the epilogue to his book: "A protective attitude by human inhabitants for the entire watershed of the Buffalo River will be mandatory if it is to survive as a beautiful clear-water stream of national significance. This will mean restrictions on industry and certain types of agriculture in the area. Such modalities we must learn to accept and live with if there be places on this earth where our descendants can know and understand the wonders of creation."

That's what Doug was up to that first summer after I met him, when, like a couple of water turtles, we were lounging along the river.

In the opening lines of this essay I mentioned that Doug and I go back to 1977 when our shared interest in art and nature found us working together on the Walter Inglis Anderson art exhibit. Artists Robert Ross, Neppie Conner, Martha Sutherland and others in the university art community were interested in having a Walter Anderson show in Fayetteville. His family was willing to loan to us works, no strings attached. This grew into plans for two galleries (October 3–22, 1977)—some work in the Arkansas Union Gallery and some in the Fine Arts Gallery.

Annie Kittrell (Arkansas Union Programs), Billie Giese (an art student), and I drove a U of A van to Ocean Springs and loaded it up with what would today be millions of dollars of art. VOILA, we had drawings, paintings, pottery, and hand-carved furniture.

Anderson was an avid birdwatcher and bird drawer. He painted birds on pottery and carved them in wood. He created huge murals with birds as central figures. We really needed a bird expert to help us interpret Anderson for the exhibits. This is where Doug came in. He showed up at the Union Gallery and began examining the art in a professorial manner.

Besides drawing and painting, Anderson wrote what he called logs, essentially a journal of his day-to-day experiences while doing the art on the Gulf islands. Doug read these logs and found phases that pertained to what was happening when Anderson was doing each watercolor. Doug collected these relevant statements and positioned them next to each of the paintings and drawings.

Besides traveling to the Gulf Coast trying to figure out Walter Anderson (and myself), I had been writing weekly feature stories for a newspaper, the *Grapevine*. Doug had seen my bird pieces. Before we were done with the Anderson exhibit, we had started talking about his state bird book project. My features tended heavy on poetic phrase and light on science. I don't know if Doug approved of them in an ornithological way, but he knew I was interested in birds and nature, and especially that I could write. That is, he saw potential in me as a collaborator on what became *Arkansas Birds* (1986).

Looking over the thirty-plus years of friendship, I can see that what happened between Doug and me over the Anderson show has been repeated with others. He has seen in many a rough-hewn graduate student potential others couldn't see; he provided opportunity for potential to flower. Off campus, he has encouraged the public to become involved in ornithology. Consider his role in founding Arkansas Audubon Society. As president of Wilson Ornithological Society, he encouraged networks between professional and nonprofessional bird enthusiasts. He helped found and then later helped resuscitate Northwest Arkansas Audubon Society.

Doug James opened his eighty-fifth year on July 25, 2010. I could go on here, but . . . Happy Birthday, Doug. After beers and cake, there's more work to do. We are glad at your being freshly minted at eighty-five, and we look forward to sharing with you the work ahead.

Charlie Wooten birding in Honey Island Swamp in Louisiana, May 1983.

Charlie

FOR A FEW interesting years, Charlie W. Wooten inhabited the wilds of western Arkansas. He came to us from Elgin, South Carolina, a rural community twenty miles outside the state capitol, Columbia.

He was a limber-limbed six-footer, with reddish hair and skin and a washtub of freckles. His southern "y'all" was not affected. He sported around in a brown Toyota named Betty Sue. Charlie presented himself as one of "them redneck country boys." Behaving like the stereotypical southerner with an RC Cola and a moon pie, he wore a green baseball cap and smoked cigarettes, thus shocking the liberal campus crowd. Though his roots were unmistakably white, southern, and rural, there was no Klansman in him, and he did not exhibit the "angry white male" syndrome so much in vogue these days.

The only member of his family to pursue higher education, Charlie came to the University of Arkansas in 1979 to study for a master's degree in zoology under Dr. Douglas A. James. He was twenty-six that year. Like the other Wooten boys, Charlie had been building houses since he was old enough to hold a hammer, a family tradition. Granddaddy Wooten had cut the virgin pine timber that grew in the rough Carolina Sandhill country around Elgin. Charlie's daddy Lem built houses on the same land. Lem prospered with help from Charlie's momma Nancy who handled the real-estate end of the family business.

Charlie inherited his love of the outdoors from Lem. Together, they fished the Wateree River east of Elgin. Trips were preceded by visits to catalpa trees where they collected their "catawba" worm bait. These velvety caterpillars of sphinx moths consume generous portions of the catalpa tree's heart-shaped leaves, gaining in this process the mass needed to make them irresistible to catfish.

Unlike others in his tribe, Charlie was infected with bird watching and the notion that he might make a living as a scientist. According to Lem, Charlie was the dreamy, lazy one of the Wooten bunch. When Charlie left home for Clemson University he didn't know what he wanted to study. To their credit, Nancy and Lem supported him in his desire not to pound nails for a living. A charismatic native of southern Louisiana named Sidney Gautreaux was teaching at Clemson when Charlie arrived. Sid is nationally respected for research in bird migration and like Charlie, proud of his southern roots. A guy named Paul Hammel was at Clemson, too, finishing his PhD research on endangered and possibly extinct Bachman's Warblers. Under their influence, Charlie earned his undergraduate degree and then headed for Fayetteville.

Dr. James hosted a graduate-student mixer at his home during Charlie's first year as a graduate student in Arkansas. Charlie leaned against the kitchen counter with an Old Milwaukee in one hand and a cigarette in the other. It was in the fall term, and there was talk of birds and thesis research. Among a small group there was also talk about football. Charlie tallied the relative merits of the Clemson Tigers versus the Arkansas Razorbacks. This drifted through beer after beer until 4 a.m. Charlie was willing to talk birds or about Clemson as long as anyone cared to stay up. At one point we adjourned outside to hoot—or I should say whistle—for Eastern Screech-Owls. This alarmed no owls, but it did bring forth the Fayetteville police.

He acquired his nickname Hootin' Wooten three months later during his first Arkansas Christmas Bird Count (CBC), an annual event in mid to late December. Some folks get up before the crack of dawn to go out looking—or rather listening for—owls. You have to hoot and whistle at them in hopes they'll respond. His hoot was so convincing that when employed in the darkness it seemed to have fooled every Barred Owl in the Ozarks. He boasted that Arkansas Barred Owls could not resist the charm of his South Carolina Wateree hoot-owl talk.

The crowd assembled in Dr. James's living room for the CBC tabulation that evening demanded he give a demonstration. Charlie was shy about performing, but at last there poured from him the soul of the great Wateree swamp forest: *HOO HOO HOOHOO . . . HOO HOO HOOHOOWL* . . . The veneration Charlie held for the Wateree transcended the material of sand, mud, turgid water, catfish, and swamp forest. You could hear it pour from his voice.

The next year, Charlie invited Fayetteville CBCers to a predawn and pre-owling party breakfast at the upstairs apartment he shared with another graduate student, Mark Schram. He promised us "Yankees" a Carolina breakfast: sausage, grits, biscuits, and eggs. When we arrived, Charlie was buried under dirty dishes, pans, skillets and cups, piled to about eye level—no kidding. This debris of previous meals was stacked in the sink, on the counter, on the stove, overflowing to the floor. Undaunted, Charlie soon had the grits boiling.

If he didn't absolutely have to be doing classroom work—either taking classes or teaching as a graduate assistant—he and Betty Sue explored distant places like the Centerton State Fish Hatchery, thirty miles north of campus. Eye to the scope, he studied shorebird migration, a Golden Guide stuck in the back pocket of his jeans. An unexpected migrant brought closer study. "Baird's Sandpiper," he exclaimed. Then, as he noted the identification in his field notebook, he called out in mock authority, "check it off."

In his two years in Arkansas he ran up forty thousand miles on Betty Sue. He saw locally rare birds, like a Tundra Swan and a *Plegadis* ibis species, at the time, neither previously reported in the Ozarks region of Arkansas. Sometimes I was invited along. He would ask if I wanted to "take a ride." If I did want to go, he would "carry me along." A "good bird" like the ibis was, in his words, "jammed-up."

During most of the time Charlie lived in Arkansas, I was working with Doug James on the book that became *Arkansas Birds*. He contributed many records of bird sightings. After he left Arkansas and returned to South Carolina, he sent back a six-page manuscript of ALL his western Arkansas bird records. He knew they would be useful in writing species accounts for the book.

During these Arkansas years, we sometimes heard about a mysterious Ruthann Royal, then living in North Carolina. She and Charlie met at a nature photography workshop on the Carolina coast. They dated a few times on his brief trips home. Ruthann had grown up in a military family. She was born in Alaska and had lived all over the country. According to Charlie, Ruthann didn't like his drinking and smoking

American Tree Sparrow along Highway 43 near Cherokee City, Benton County, Arkansas, during stormy weather of February 8, 2011.

and his tendency to overdo the redneck bit. She was interested in the naturalist behind these habits, but she wasn't in a hurry to marry.

Meanwhile, Charlie had many Arkansas friends. Like Ruthann, we all shared his interest in natural history. For all of Charlie's redneck posturing, including sexist jokes, he found independent, nontraditional people attractive. At least three of us went on to get our own advanced degrees in zoology, with a special focus on birds. We all shared his interests in natural history, especially turtles, snakes, and salamanders.

For his master's research he chose a study area in the Wedington Unit of the Ozark National Forest, west of Fayetteville. He experimented with methods to accurately census birds nesting in the wooded hills and ravines. Local high school kids had previously discovered this woodland. Charlie was experimenting with the best ways to census birds; they were also experimenting. On more than one occasion he found the telltale signs of romantic endeavor, condoms flung out a window and lodged in a cedar. Thereafter, his study site acquired a nickname very much in the Charliesque vein of humor—French Tickler Hollow.

Veterans like Charlie know their woodland birds by voice. Out at Wedington he knew the buzzy *zoo-zoo-zoo-zoo-zeeee* up in the canopy was a Northern Parula without even looking. He recognized the Wood Thrush's fluting performed from a dogwood down in the hollow. The birds of French Tickler Hollow became the focus of his life here. He tramped miles back and forth through humid woods, measuring trees and shrubs and counting plants while swatting biting flies and pulling ticks off his legs.

Wedington became an Arkansas version of the Wateree. He found Barred Owls roughly equal to those of the Carolina swamp forests. He discovered a nest of that seldom seen but often heard southern night singer, Chuck-will's-widow. He became familiar with the Wild Turkey's early morning gobble.

Charlie Wooten's summer birds
Wedington Unit, Ozark National Forest
Washington County, Arkansas in 1980–1981

Wild Turkey*	Red-eyed Vireo
Great Blue Heron*	Blue Jay
Turkey Vulture*	American Crow*
Cooper's Hawk*	Purple Martin*
Broad-winged Hawk*	Carolina Chickadee
Yellow-billed Cuckoo	Tufted Titmouse
Eastern Screech-Owl*	White-breasted Nuthatch
Great Horned Owl*	Blue-gray Gnatcatcher
Barred Owl	Wood Thrush
Chuck-will's-widow*	Northern Parula
Chimney Swift*	Black-and-white Warbler
Ruby-throated Hummingbird	Worm-eating Warbler
Red-bellied Woodpecker	Ovenbird
Downy Woodpecker	Kentucky Warbler
Hairy Woodpecker	Yellow-breasted Chat
Pileated Woodpecker*	Summer Tanager
Eastern Wood-Pewee	Scarlet Tanager
Acadian Flycatcher	Northern Cardinal
Great Crested Flycatcher	Indigo Bunting
White-eyed Vireo	Brown-headed Cowbird
Yellow-throated Vireo	American Goldfinch

Denotes flying over study site.

In January 1982, after his degree was safely finished, he quietly organized and printed at his own expense a tongue-in-cheek magazine of satire and humor called *The Arkansas Naturalist*. The title explained that the magazine was "Published by the Arkansas Society of Systematic and Ecological Stuff," abbreviated A.S.S.E.S.

Charlie (and others who contributed articles) poked fun at birders and government in general. He shared with other scientists a deep anger at the Reagan administration's crusade against environmental protection. This is reflected in the lead article of the *Naturalist*, written in the flood tide of Reagan's attempted trashing of environmental laws. Dedicated to President Reagan, "a true environmentalist and conservationist," it called for the wholesale extermination of endangered species. "After a new species has been described," Charlie wrote, "steps should be taken to wipe it off the face of this planet. These measures would cut down drastically on the complexity of biology . . . save money . . ." etc.

Charlie could also poke fun at himself. A full-page illustration in the *Naturalist* featured an unshaven, unkempt, and unmistakably Charliesque character with a baseball cap and Clemson Tigers T-shirt. This guy was swilling down beer under a tree with a sign that read "Breeding Birds Register Here." Breeding Bird Surveyors, take note! The *Naturalist* marked the end of his Arkansas years.

In May 1982, I went over to his upstairs apartment to help him move. We packed his Betty Sue with telescope, binoculars, two weeks of dirty laundry, and twenty boxes of books and ornithological journals. Charlie usually wore jeans, no matter what the weather, but today he was in cut-off shorts. I saw an enormous scar on one leg.

Seven years before he'd had an operation for melanoma. There had been no recurrence. Now back in Carolina, master of science degree in hand, he moved in with his family and took up the family trade, pounding nails. He even went to church a few times with Ruthann. But the old Charlie was still around. He sent me a bumper sticker that read, "IT TAKES A STUD TO BUILD A HOUSE."

He plunged into independent bird studies in the Carolina Sandhills and drafted a small bird book like the one he helped me produce, titled *Birds of the Western Arkansas Ozarks*. Pounding nails paid his bills and gave him some relief from the academic life, but it was a temporary

Charlie's Wooten's drawing of the Wooten easy method for a Breeding Bird Survey. Published in his satirical magazine, *The Arkansas Naturalist,* in January 1982.

expedient. He applied and was accepted into Clemson University's PhD program.

He and Ruthann married in 1984. A daughter, Ellen, came along in 1985. In order to finance his doctoral program, Charlie obtained a grant from the Forest Service to study Red-cockaded Woodpeckers. Unfortunately, his research plan never meshed with the goals of his Clemson doctoral committee. They wanted him to test theories; Charlie wanted to be out in nature where he could more casually think and explore like he had done at Wedington. The committee rejected his first two research proposals. A third rejection would have been the end of his career in academics. His years of dreaming and study now came down to preparing an acceptable proposal.

Of course, there were other choices. He could have been an outstanding conservationist or naturalist anywhere. He could have managed a wildlife refuge or perhaps gone to work directly for an agency like the U.S. Forest Service, then stepping up work for recovery of endangered Red-cockaded Woodpeckers. However, his role models for a life outside Elgin had been professors. He had his heart set on academic life. In the world of academics, a PhD is the big union card. Success at Clemson mattered a lot.

His letters at this time were half-filled with family matters, including the latest from Ellen and Ruthann, his exhilaration at birding along the Carolina coast and working with a bunch of hotshot birders around Clemson. The other half was pain. He found himself in a crunch that many graduate students face. Turning a love for natural history into a professional skill that could make a living is an ideal that does not always mesh with the mission of modern research-oriented universities.

Charlie wanted to study the whole outdoors. Strictly theoretical research was a lot like pounding nails. The possible outcomes of such effort seemed less certain than house building.

"Science is going through a lot of soul-searching, particularly behavioral ecology," he wrote. "Scientists tend to think in terms of black-and-white and often avoid the colored areas on the fringes (often termed variance or noise). There are many attempts to generate and test various laws and theories to make our field more like the 'hard sciences' of physics and chemistry. I think it is a futile search. There are many ways to solve the same problem when life is responding to the environment."

It was a depressing time. Ruthann said later he spent a lot of time in front of the tube watching game shows. But he'd also been doing a lot of thinking. Maybe he was moving toward resolution, a breaking-out from his bottleneck.

He called from Elgin in the fall of 1986. "Hey there, buddy, what's happenin'?" It was his old characteristic greeting. It wasn't a happy call, though. After his second research proposal was rejected, he, Ruthann and Ellen had returned to Elgin where his choices were to pound nails or teach high-school math. Charlie chose math while working on a third proposal.

During the summer he had a bad stomachache that was at first diagnosed as an ulcer. This made sense, after all. The pressure at Clemson was unbearable. Treatments for an ulcer didn't help. Exploratory surgery revealed a recurrence of melanoma. There were friends in Fayetteville he wanted me to contact. Then we talked birds.

A Snowy Owl had been seen only six miles from his house. Did I want to see it? I wanted to make another birding trip with my South Carolina buddy, but by the time I flew out there, Charlie couldn't travel and the Snowy Owl was gone. His brothers had thoughtfully put big brush piles conveniently outside a window where he could watch winter birds. There were feeders in the yard. We talked birds in the house. He loaned me his winter coat so I could walk in the Carolina Sandhills.

Alert to the end, he passed away in December 1986. Ruthann subsequently took an ornithology course. She and Ellen went birding where, Ruthann said, Ellen seemed to be taking up where her daddy left off.

It's probably not obvious if you see me on the street, but Charlie owns a vivid part of me. Twenty-five years after his passing, I'm next to him as he looks through his scope at "jammed up" birds and a celebration begins. It's a small flock Upland Sandpipers in a grassy field near Centerton. I'm out there on the Honey Island Swamp in Louisiana, dreaming with him of Ivory-billed Woodpeckers. Surely, one will fly over us if we just wait long enough. We're on our backs in the grass on the Texas coast, looking straight up into a swarm of northward bound Broad-winged Hawks. Time doesn't bracket such reality.

He was not the first ardent birder whose interests paralleled my own. That person would be Walter Inglis Anderson, the now-famous Mississippi artist. But Anderson passed in 1965 during the time in my life when I had not yet even ever heard the term "bird watcher." Through his published journals and paintings, I came to know his interest and devotion to birds and natural history. And it was through this interest in Anderson that I got to know ornithologist Doug James several years before Charlie became Doug's student. These developing interests were coming together in the 1970s, pointing the direction I was headed, though I didn't then recognize it.

We were not ready to let Charlie go when he moved from Fayetteville back home to South Carolina. We sure weren't ready to let him go in his death. His Fayetteville friends set up a scholarship fund in his name.

Common Grackle with crawfish at the state fish hatchery in Centerton, Benton County, Arkansas, on March 8, 2011.

Contributions ranging from $5 to $100 eventually brought this amount to $1,200. This was not a large amount of money, even in the 1980s, but it was something. The idea was that in this way we could share in Charlie's future—that is, in Ruthann and Ellen.

Ruthann finished a master's degree in library science in 1992, and has worked since as a public-school librarian. She didn't lose the interest in photography that she and Charlie shared in their first meeting. But increasingly, she focused on supporting herself and Ellen. She told me, only half-joking, that over the years she has mostly taken photographs of Ellen.

Charlie has been gone over two decades and Ellen graduated near the top of her Columbia College class in Columbia, South Carolina. Columbia College, by the way, is near where Charlie grew up. And like her father, Ellen is a huge fan of the Clemson Tigers, following football and baseball. She peppers her conversations with statistics about players and teams, attends games, and has been to recent Tiger bowl games.

This reminds me of standing around drinking Old Milwaukees with Charlie at Doug James's, the conversation lurching toward relative merits of Tigers and Arkansas Razorbacks. She's also a big fan of what she terms, "awesome blue-skied sunshiney days!"

I picked up that last statement from Ellen. Her blogging demonstrates a maturing intellect, including self-deprecating humor and Charliesque complexities. On her blog page she lists, among other interests, "learning everything, reading anything, running . . . traveling . . . taking pictures, and following Christ." She cites as expertise "packing suitcases, arm-chair coaching, making microwave pizza, doodling, keeping the room from getting too clean . . ." etc.

Her posting for October 9, 2005, contained ironic humor as she alternately twists and sorts her sports passion when pitted against the humanity of Clemson's sports rivals, the Gamecocks at University of South Carolina (USC): "You know, I really don't like USC fans that are civil. It leaves me confused. We're supposed to be big bad rivals, no? Hate each other's guts?" Then, "So honestly, what do I say to the Gamecock fan who sits behind me at church telling me he'll be cheering for the Tigers on Thursday?" It reminds me a lot of Charlie's *Arkansas Naturalist*.

Humor is mixed with the serious. "I don't think everything happens for a reason," she writes on October 26, 2005. "It's a popular idea right now, but I don't think a parent dying of cancer . . . is what God intended to happen necessarily . . . I think it comes down to what you believe about our will—is everything already written? What I'm about to have for lunch included? I personally believe . . . that God orchestrates the big things . . . I believe that God could use my lunch today for his bigger plan if he wanted, but I also believe we have room to move . . ."

Ruthann has told me that four and one-half-years passed from the time she and Charlie met at the photography workshop until they married. He wrote her steadily, sharing with her his dreams and adventures. She has saved these letters, a future treasure trove for Ellen. I have a picture of Charlie holding Ellen. I think it comes from the time before Charlie knew he was sick. To quote Charlie, it's a "jammed up" thing to see them together.

I got to know Charlie at what I'd term a Lewis and Clark level: we were explorers. We were dreaming the dreams of youth, before our chance to make a mark. A whole new world lay before us.

American Robins enjoying persimmons after an ice storm in Fayetteville on January 27, 2009.

Yard Birds

MY DAUGHTER ARIEL would have been Phoebe or Robin if it had been up to me. And it's not that Ariel is not a fine name, it's just that by the time she fledged from Springdale Hospital on January 18, 1985, her mother Nancy Edelman wasn't comfortable with giving her a bird name. And it wasn't that she disliked birds. Things had just become altogether too birdy for her.

In the years before Ariel, Nancy had enjoyed raising an orphan American Robin. "Peeps" was blown from its nest in a dogwood tree during an early May thunderstorm. Then as now, Nancy was completely comfortable leaning against a log in the woods, among bugs and birds. She just never got into the "binocular thing" and its corollary, ritualistic recitations of formal bird names according to the American Ornithologists' Union. The extensive paraphernalia of field biology was not part of Nancy's universe. A one-on-one relationship was her "thing," and Peeps thrived and returned to the wild under her care.

Ariel came at a time when I was way over-the-top bird crazy. Here's how I argued my case for giving her a bird name: American Robins are common in the yard, whose nest is just bound to be the first seen and likely source of blue eggs that mark western Arkansas springs. Their dawn choruses fill our town. Phoebes sing *phoebe-phoebe* from rock bluffs along the Buffalo River, under the bridge over Lee Creek at Devil's Den State Park, and from country porches. It's a voice of the wilds. Nancy didn't see it that way. She did not own binoculars or a Peterson Field Guide. Yet, mystifying to the bird-lister in me, she enjoyed the outdoors.

I hadn't myself spent a lot of time imaging being a father. On the other hand, a new joy was kicking within Nancy. As I wrote species accounts for a bird book, she wondered if the apartment would be large enough for a family. I was in the field looking for Lapland Longspurs

Ariel Neal and her mother, Nancy Edelman, on the porch in Fayetteville, summer 1988.

among flocks of Horned Larks. It barely registered in my head that a human child, in part my creation, was about to enter my life.

I was wondering if my bird book would ever be published. That child who would be Ariel—but not Robin and not Phoebe—was stretching inside Nancy.

Ariel seemed ready for birth on a mild midwinter day. The temperature was warm when we went into the hospital. That all changed when a storm roared into northern Arkansas. Nancy had a long night of labor. Outside, the world turned into ice and snow. That harsh weather brought us flocks of American Tree Sparrows. And as the storm was ending, Ariel herself was making the big migration. As things turned out, I too was making a big migration.

Ariel's first view of the world was mostly white, a wintry wonderland. It was a wild time—new parents and a new being. Birds driven by hunger from the fields were dark masses in the universal white. As we headed home with Ariel, flocks of Eastern Meadowlarks and Savannah Sparrows foraged the highway shoulder for seeds fallen from chicken feed trucks.

Ariel was tucked away in a car seat, swaddled in a dense cocoon of blankets. Tiny dark eyes peered at the amazing world. I was struggling with what we would do when we got home with our daughter. I could identify birds, but I couldn't identify myself as a father.

Ariel was conceived in the springtime of 1984. Masses of white serviceberry blossoms were conspicuous in the grayish, mostly leafless Ozark forest during late March. Serviceberry or "sarvis" initiates our mountain spring. That was the spring of the Lesser Goldfinch at Art Evans's place in Benton County—then, the only record for Arkansas. I found a dying Short-eared Owl wing-trapped on a barbed wire fence during a trip to my mother's in Booneville on March 23. There were at least twenty-seven Yellow-headed Blackbirds and a dozen Upland Sandpipers at Centerton in Benton County on April 24. There were hundreds of Pine Siskins in Evergreen Cemetery near the U of A campus in Fayetteville on April 25. Pawpaws were blooming along the Buffalo River in the first week of May. In short, life was moving forward—a lot more and at a faster pace than I imagined.

A finale of sorts came on May 6: "BIG FALLOUT DAY!" is what I wrote in my field notes, much like a newspaper headline. "Stormed all night, lightning, thunder, rain. Woke this morning, hear BUZZES right outside the bedroom. Birds singing in every tree. Have to go to the store, so walk not to miss anything. Ovenbird under a yaupon bush, Swainson's Thrushes on the sidewalk, Tennessee Warblers in the spreading oaks. I identify one bird and 10 fly from the same tree. Takes a long time to get groceries. Now home, eat, walked to the cemetery, which is remarkably alive. Birds birds birds–15 species of warblers and how many more? Painted Buntings singing in the middle of town."

It was a big spring migration. By then, Ariel, too, had become more than merely her mother's dream. A person might think—I did think at the time—that fatherhood would be the end of such things. That is, a father would not have time for birding.

My friend Eleanor Johnson, Ariel's godmother, raised a son and daughter in Fayetteville. Starting in the 1950s, they wrote notes about birds in the page margins of a Golden Guide—the one by Herbert Zim and Ira Gabrielson. Over the years El and her kids logged dates next to many of the 129 species illustrated in color. El's husband, Tommy, taught botany at the university. It was a time when people did without cars; they didn't own one. Tommy walked to campus, which was two blocks away. El and the kids kept track of flowers, snakes, spiders, and birds in the yard. Naturally, all birds noted in the Golden Guide were literally yard birds.

Ariel's godmother, Eleanor Johnson, in front of her home in Fayetteville in 1989. She and her children kept lists of birds, frogs, snakes, and interesting bugs in their yard.

Like the Johnsons, I did without a car in the years before Ariel. The ten-speed bicycle was my answer to America's insatiable appetite for movement. I was just sure that sensible people concerned about air pollution, energy shortages, and oil wars would choose the bicycle. Bicycling was a refreshing belief among folks in their twenties in America, especially those who didn't have children and didn't commute miles to work.

I did try hauling Ariel around in a special bicycle seat. The bike with baby just didn't balance that well when I suddenly stopped and piled off to see that Orange-crowned Warbler in the bushes. Soon I developed a healthy respect for cars. Nancy was commuting to work in Springdale. There were catbirds and cardinals in our yard, but I could find many more birds via automobile.

Ariel's first official birding trip came at age two weeks: February 3, 1985. Winter ice remained. The proud new parents toured all around Fayetteville with baby Ariel snuggled in her car seat. We visited Lake Sequoyah and Lake Fayetteville: 235 Mallards stood on the frozen lake. We peered briefly at a Great Horned Owl in a big sycamore tree out in a pasture. Yellow eyes and ear tufts rose above the bulky nest of sticks; we didn't see downy young. We did see juncos and White-throated Sparrows along the Farmington road. That's not a bad list for a kid sixteen days old.

Ariel's second birding trip came on February 15. Like Great Horned

Owls, Great Blue Herons nest early in the year. Adult herons claim nests in the tall cottonwoods and sycamores of river bottoms in the months otherwise considered winter. We took a ride out into the Illinois River bottomlands east of Tontitown. There in the big sycamores and cottonwoods was a treetop rookery of about fifty nests, easily viewed from the highway.

On February 20 we drove out to brushy fields on the north side of Lake Fayetteville to see male American Woodcocks perform their aerial courtship dancing. We watched from the car adjacent the environmental study center.

Ariel got a look at her first rare bird on March 8. We drove up to Highfill in Benton County. Joyce Shedell had a Common Redpoll at her feeder. We sat in her kitchen and soon had the bird in view—one of a very few records for Arkansas.

We birded steadily all through Ariel's first spring. On April 4 we caught the Yellow-throated Warbler migration in a campground alongside Lee Creek at Devil's Den. We marveled at white blooms on the May Apples. On April 13, we saw two Greater Scaups at Lake Fayetteville. Ariel had her first natural history excursion in a backpack on April 14, when we hit the dogwood blooming peak in the Illinois River bottomlands. Ariel rode in a backpack with me May 3 during a state meeting of Arkansas Audubon Society. This included a field trip I led to the Wedington Unit of the Ozark National Forest. With Ariel still in the car seat, we counted 118 Stilt Sandpipers at Centerton on May 14 and 183 White-rumped Sandpipers there on May 28.

An overnight trip to my mother's home in Booneville on May 25–26 yielded Cerulean Warblers at Cherry Bend in the Ozark National Forest and Painted Buntings at Booneville. We went right through the summer into fall and caught the Buff-breasted Sandpiper migration at the University Farm in Fayetteville on September 7. Ariel was nearing eight months at that point.

Our "yard" became any place in western Arkansas accessible by a car, binoculars, telescope, or backpack. I learned on the job that if your profession is birding and new-fathering, it's often easy to care for a baby daughter in a Toyota.

Of course it's true Ariel could not regurgitate the daily list of these trips in a veteran birder's lingo, but she sure enjoyed the rides, excitement, and being with her folks. She happily napped as I meticulously counted sandpipers and cranked my neck upwards to see ceruleans high in the crowns of red oaks. I learned by experience to pack the field guides AND juice, animal crackers, and bananas.

We went to see nesting Great Horned Owls and Great Blue Herons, but they weren't the only creatures nesting. We were nesting, too.

The University of Arkansas Press published *Arkansas Birds,* with Douglas A. James and Joseph C. Neal as coauthors, in December 1986. That's just about a year after Ariel's debut. My labors on *Arkansas Birds* involved years of research, composition on a manual typewriter, and much literal cutting and pasting of changes in the text. I probably poured a case of white out over my many typing mistakes—two-fingered typing and a lot of new stuff learned about birds. Finally, there was the birth of a new book: at 8½ x 11 in size, 3.5 pounds, 402 pages, and 366 bird species.

This was a time when social weight accorded the coauthor of such a heavy book of science encouraged me to think *Arkansas Birds* was the key for me to understand the meaning of life. It was, after all, a man's work and a visible accomplishment. In my world of the time, this had mass and gravitational pull, at least in certain universes.

With *Arkansas Birds* in hand, my dear mother, Hazel Kennedy Neal, had a kind of bulletproof, socially acceptable evidence that her son had turned out OK at last, despite contrary views in our family. She had suffered through my years as hippie-poet-dreamer and worker of menial jobs that lacked the gravity accorded authors of heavy science books. Too bad my father had been too long gone to experience the autograph party and bragging rights accorded an author's parents. I say these things humorously—but you know what I mean. It was there, on the cover—my name—and inside, my picture.

Someday, if my mother had her way, it would be inscribed on my tombstone "HE WAS COAUTHOR OF ARKANSAS BIRDS." In case you don't get my drift here, that actually translates as, "HE IS NOT JUST A DAMN HIPPIE."

Yet, for the indisputable value of such an effort, the book became somewhat dated almost immediately. As news spread around the Arkansas birding community that Doug and I were actually finishing the book, new information rushed ahead in a torrent. It hasn't stopped.

Within five years, Arkansas birders had found ten bird species NEVER before recorded in the state, and therefore not part of the text in our 1986 book. It started out in eastern Arkansas with a Royal Tern at Lonoke in 1986 and it continues today. By 2011 the state list tops four hundred species.

Note for Arkansas birders: don't despair. This is the fertile soil of a new book.

As Ariel grew, my days of flat-out, all day, bird-hard birding waned. I enjoyed lying in a hammock with her. As she napped, I watched a Northern Flicker forage for hackberries, hanging from the end of a dangling bough, precariously it seemed. I listened more intently to male and female Northern Cardinals.

The robin chorus at dawn reminded me I was a birder, but now I was sharing my home with a daughter, in our own nest. For that reason, I did not chase the Black-throated Green Warblers found nesting in the Ozark National Forest. I did not chase the state's first record for Yellow-billed Loon, discovered by Mike Mlodinow at Beaver Lake Dam in November 1991. Ditto for a Black-legged Kittiwake, found at the same time—northwestern Arkansas's only record.

Ariel turned six as Arkansas ornithology marched ever onward. Meanwhile, her mother and I fought, separated, and eventually divorced. Parenting now included fresh challenges and unexpected rewards.

The former bird-hard super birder and bird book writer began to fade. In its place, I noticed Ariel's favorite toys, and made sure they were packed in the car on occasional trips to the state fish hatchery at Centerton. I took her and friends swimming at the Ponca low-water bridge over the Buffalo River, and listened for American Redstarts and Wood Thrushes while they jumped into the clear cold water. Trips to see Grandma Neal at Booneville offered me a golden opportunity: Mom wanted to play with her granddaughter. While they played, I explored Ouachita Mountain farmland for Painted Buntings. This is now called multitasking.

Me as "Daddy bird" was a big hit at Ariel's preschool. I had a box full of bird nests, bird eggs, feathers, colorful African stamps featuring birds, a couple of left over bird-feather Halloween masks, and an Ostrich egg. Ariel was my proud helper, passing the stuff out among her classmates.

The egg suffered what was then termed a "booboo." It was dropped and became five pieces. But preschools are places where things get regularly broken. The kids got bandaids and soon had the egg back together. Booboo egg soared in popularity.

Ariel wasn't even four, and already she was an enthusiastic swimmer. Just give her a bathing suit and some water, and we were bound to have a good time. So, after her pre-school and my workday, we headed for the Buffalo River. It was early September. We drove right to the Ponca low-water bridge. The Buffalo was clear as an aquarium. We saw a big fish that turned out to be a northern hog sucker. The banks were lined with a thick grove of brilliant, blooming cardinal flowers. A few fall leaves were drifting down.

After some swimming and some flower admiring, we drove over to the Lost Valley campground—had it ALL to ourselves. We never saw another soul until Saturday afternoon. At dusk we shared Lost Valley with lots of bats, and in the fall night sky we looked for the wishing star. A Whip-poor-will sang briefly in that dusk—unusual relatively late in the season. Ariel found the wishing star while I was listening.

I heard a screech-owl, imitated their calls, and soon had two in the air near us and a few more calling. Perhaps this was a family group? Later, there was lots of hooting by Barred Owls. These were mostly *who all* calls and just a few *who cooks for you?* Ariel hooted back pretty good, but she was soon back to wishing stars.

I woke in the middle of a fabulously bright starry night. The heavens seemed unexpectedly generous with all varieties of wishing stars. I could see stars and stars, and stars seemed to decorate the boughs of trees like so many celestial Christmas lights.

Ariel woke too, needing to pee. Said she was afraid to go out of the tent since a wolf might get her. I told her not to worry about wolves, but she had better worry about dinosaurs. She knows what happened to dinosaurs, so out she went, but not before mentioning foxes. Foxes don't bother little girls, I assured her, and out she went into the wishing star night.

Ariel kept me closer to home. In time I learned that yard birds are far more plentiful than I imagined. In place of flat-out all-day marches

American Robin nestlings about ready to fledge at Fayetteville in May 2009.

of birding-to-the-death, I noticed the big overflights of Snow Geese, plainly heard and seen from our yard. In place of hundreds of miles of driving to document a rare bird, there was satisfaction in hearing fall's first White-throated Sparrow in our honeysuckle-covered sideyard, just beyond the hammock. During spring migration I saw a brilliant male Chestnut-sided Warbler at Gregory Park, right behind a Fayetteville McDonald's where we'd gone for an ice cream cone.

There were mysterious sounds in the late summer night. I eventually recognized Upland Sandpipers making their southward migration over our yard. There was a big lazy spiral of American White Pelicans one day when we were swinging at Wilson Park. I watched Blue Jays collecting pecans while waiting for Ariel at Washington Elementary.

Ariel and I worked together on a study of a robin's nest we found in the yard. Where did the robin collect material we saw in the nest? How did the nest fit together? What does this say about robin habitat selection? She put it together for her elementary school science fair. She took a blue ribbon for her project. Robins still nest in the yard.

During those years my birding was measured in half hours rather than days, in city blocks rather than miles, in a little satisfaction rather than the flat-out exaltation of a huge trip with super birders and hundreds of interesting birds, and the constant birder talk of such trips. I hauled Ariel and friends to the skating rink, movies, and birthday parties. There were regular sleepovers at our house. If the Fayetteville Christmas Bird Count fell on a day when Ariel and friends needed to go to a party, I missed all or part of the count. I did make most of the counts, however, thanks to Ariel's mom and friends.

Many questions were on my mind as Ariel grew. The evolution of my own birding style stimulated a search for perspective. If birding requires lots of commitment, what value is derived? Is it merely a reckless blowing of time, energy, and money, or does it serve a wider purpose? Where does it fit into life's broader flow?

I had a chance to go to graduate school, but it would involve being away from home for part of the year. I would be studying for a master's degree. Eventually I could help manage an endangered bird, the Red-cockaded Woodpecker, on the Ouachita National Forest. My office on the forest would be at Waldron, near Booneville, where mother lived. Birds and a great opportunity called, but it would pull me away from the little bird, Ariel. I had a lot to think about.

Mitzi was a graduate student in fisheries when we met. She was a born cut-up, cute, athletic, her brown hair in tight coils, Afro-style. She bounced around like the cheerleader she had been in high school. She had a son, then age ten, and a daughter who like Ariel was six. She and her husband were running on an end-of-marriage track, parallel to the one inhabited by Nancy and me. Sometimes her daughter Rachael came up to the campus, standing behind Mitzi, her soft brown eyes peeking from between her mother's legs. Mitzi was one year ahead of me in graduate school.

Mitzi and I liked gardening. I knew someone with a chicken house twenty miles east of Fayetteville. We went out there, loaded up ten bags of litter, piled it in the car, and headed back. My car had no AC. With the windows down, fifty-five miles per hour began sucking litter out of the open bags. Airborne in the car, it grew into a furious, stinking, white tornado. It sure made marigolds and our relationship bloom.

When Mitzi graduated, we loaded up a big van, and she and the kids left for Mount Ida in the Ouachita Mountains, three and one-half hours south of Fayetteville. She was starting her career as a fisheries biologist on the Ouachita National Forest.

My divorce from Nancy, plus Mitzi's move, made for complex weekends. Not every weekend, but on occasion I would pick up Ariel after school, buzz by our apartment for clothes and snacks, then head two hours south for an overnight stop at my mother's place in Booneville. We would be there at least long enough for Mom to take Ariel dress shopping at Walmart. Then it was on to Mount Ida, a further two hours south, to catch up with Mitzi and her kids. We would all go swimming in the Ouachita River. Finally, after an overnight, Ariel and I strapped in for a straight drive back to Fayetteville, three and one-half hours, in time for school.

My own graduation a year later came with an invitation to join the woodpecker business at Waldron. Home number one would remain in Fayetteville with Ariel. In terms of my province, Waldron would become a second home. From Waldron it was thirty minutes one way to Mom in Booneville, and that would become a third home. Finally, home number four was one hour in a different direction from Waldron, to Mitzi and Mount Ida.

With my professional career underway in the Ouachitas, Sunday became a day of parting. It meant starting at the Fayetteville apartment by gathering up Ariel, plus some of her toys and clothes. I was neither ready for us to leave the apartment nor to say goodbye to Ariel at Nancy's. Dropping off Ariel at her mother's was a painful reminder that we three no longer shared a nest. On such evenings, I was an emotionally disembodied figure, heading south to a future whose meaning was unclear to me.

In Booneville Mother would have a yard that needed mowing. While I was mowing, she would be in the kitchen making dinner. She wasn't healthy, so the cooking and after-dinner cleaning was a big effort. But it connected us to a past—when I was a boy and my father was alive and we were all at home together. You could taste it in her gravy and pot roast. You could feel it in the small talk about what my sisters and their families were up to in Georgia and Florida. She had a bedroom for me and wanted me to stay over, and I did sometimes, but

Mitzi and her family were out there and expected me. I wanted to see them, too.

With a few lame excuses and lots of backward glances, I was off to Mount Ida and what seemed a promising future. I often drove the hour trip to Mitzi's after work in Waldron. She wanted my opinions about a house. It could be big enough for all of us, including Ariel. We walked around the ten acres with big shortleaf pines and oaks. Wood Thrushes were singing and I could hear inviting *p-tucks* of Summer Tanagers. The house had a big country porch, with a swing that Ariel and Rachael really liked. A phoebe was nesting under the eave. The asking price was attractive and Mitzi, a good bargainer, thought we could get it for less. It was doable.

Lying there with Mitzi that night, we talked about work, but inside I was alone with trouble. Ariel and Rachael were effectively sisters. As professional biologists, Mitzi and I had a lot in common. Maybe I could move Ariel to Mount Ida? If I tried to move Ariel to Mount Ida, where would this leave Nancy? I couldn't imagine Nancy agreeing to such an arrangement. I couldn't imagine even asking her to make such a choice.

My mother's condition deteriorated, and I flew with her to Florida where she could live with my youngest sister's family. This flight was the last time I would see her. She said to me, "Keep Ariel first." It was an echo from her own past when she herself was a young woman, divorced, with my sisters to raise, and trying to figure out how to be a mother midst the unsettled condition of her life.

"Keep Ariel first," reverberated in my mind. How could I do this? I found that despite being divorced, I retained loyalty to Nancy. I could not justify in my mind attempting to separate Ariel from her. Call it guilt on my part because of the break-up of our marriage, or something else, but as surely as the iceberg that found the Titanic, my reluctance to move Ariel tore a fatal hole in the effort to create a new family with Mitzi. As our relationship faltered, I made a down payment on a house just big enough for Ariel and me, in Fayetteville.

Rachael paid us a visit, jumping with Ariel on a new trampoline in our yard. Mitzi had found a solid guy who had loyalties mainly to his career in the Forest Service and no children of his own. He was ready to make his number-one home with Mitzi and her children. Eventually they would have children of their own.

This outcome was a hard pill for me to swallow, but it's impossible to argue with the logic. I have not regretted Mom's advice: Keep Ariel first. It was her last lesson in rearing me, and a good one, too.

Ariel and I had many of those Sunday nights when we said goodbye as I dropped her at Nancy's. It was very difficult, especially when she was little. With a sinking heart, I headed south early on Monday mornings. It was hard to commit myself to making the turn south onto the highway. I could turn back, couldn't I? Couldn't I just choose another direction for my life? Wasn't I a horrible person for leaving Fayetteville and a daughter, for woodpeckers in Waldron? Years later, I still have no firm answers. Perhaps there aren't any.

I passed isolated lights of farmhouses deep and dark in the mountains. The darkness dredged up ghosts inside me, reminded me of many failings. Failings filled me with regret. I thought of my father, Grover Ray Neal, and all the traveling around he did trying to make a living. What would he do? I thought of the failure of my marriage to Ariel's mother. I thought of my mother cooking for me in Booneville and her death in Florida. I just wanted to turn around and go home. I wanted to shut off the feelings, to hug my daughter and make it all go away. I wanted back in the hammock of her childhood, when—in retrospect at least—things were more sensible. Then I would see a car light at one of these farmhouses.

They too go to work, to dreams, to obligations. They too live with their successes and failures. They maybe drive further to their work and toward their destinies, and their journeys may be harder. How am I to know? And finally midst such bleakness and hopelessness in my spirit, there would be a crack of dawn. Fayetteville was thirty miles behind me. It seemed best to go forward. The Ouachita Mountains, and a future, lay ahead.

I was clearing some old file folders recently. There were drafts of hundreds of pages for *Arkansas Birds*. Always a recycler—always a little guilty about using so much paper—I'd saved the old drafts of the book's species accounts. Why did I still have these, twenty years after publication? I soon discovered that the papers in the file weren't saved for recycling.

Ariel's tiny bare-foot prints in green grace the blank back of the page where I'd written the Bald Eagle species account. The Turkey Vulture account featured small feet and toes in lime. There were brown and green tiny feet on the opposite side of the Sharp-shinned Hawk account.

It was a rainy day long ago when we did these paintings. We were playing that day. We spread all those species accounts on the floor. Ariel walked through blobs of bright color.

August 2010: This Arkansas birder is back from a late-July–early-August trip to Delaware Bay, near where the broad Delaware River pours into the Atlantic Ocean, between Lewes, Delaware, and Cape May, New Jersey. I was out there at the invitation of Ariel; her mother and my former wife, Nancy; and her grandparents on her mother Nancy's side, Margaret and Arnold Edelman. The Edelmans own a house at Broadkill Beach.

The yard has clumps of wax myrtle shrubs and a tidal creek through Prime Hook National Wildlife Refuge, a complex of marshes associated with the Delaware and the Atlantic. Yard birds include Seaside Sparrows with Greater Black-backed Gulls patrolling the air.

Lewes and Cape May are famous among birders because it is here, in May, when horseshoe crabs come ashore to lay eggs. It is here where much of the world's population of Red Knots fuel their annual migration of over nine thousand miles on crab eggs.

Here's the not-so-surprising headline: "Birder from Arkansas Enthralled by Common Birds" in this place of ecological wealth. Of course I love the Red-eyed Vireos and Painted Buntings of Arkansas, but I simultaneously crave what seems exotic: Clapper Rails chasing fiddler crabs across mudflats exposed at low tide. I spent a lot of time in the Edelman's yard, watching this ancient dance of rising and falling water, predator (rail) and prey (crab), and the manner in which moons and suns seem expansive over a sea of densely green marsh grass.

At twenty-five, Ariel is reaching her stride. After graduating from Fayetteville High School, she moved out to the Pacific Northwest and eventually settled in Portland, Oregon, far from immediate family. I still live in Fayetteville, and her mother lives in Ashland, Virginia. But in December 2009 Ariel traveled out to Ashland for Nancy's birthday, and in April 2010, she traveled to Fayetteville for mine.

Ariel Neal with her grandmother, Margaret Edelman, on the Lewes–Cape May Ferry at the mouth of the Delaware River in August 2010.

Here's the personal headline: Nancy and I divorced twenty years ago, but we never used Ariel as weapon in our marriage dissolution. Ariel hasn't had to pretend to take sides. There has been the assumption that ties between families could continue. That's why Ariel felt comfortable inviting me to Broadkill Beach, with support from her grandmother Margaret.

When Ariel was little, we lay in a hammock together and listened to birds out in our yard. I led birding field trips with her in a backpack. Later, I loaded up the back seat of our car with toys and snacks and she played with Barbies while I scanned shorebirds at the state fish hatchery.

Inviting me to Broadkill Beach, she knew her bird-watching dad would spend as much time as possible out in the yard watching rails. Ariel brought Ian, her boyfriend. She wanted him to meet all of her family in a relaxed environment.

I did see a Whimbrel and a White Ibis, but the real headline is how life moves forward, like tides and the moon's phases. Ian is a fine Scrabble player, and this went down well with Ariel's Scrabble-playing family.

Male Yellow-headed Blackbird in roadside marsh habitat near the Siloam Springs airport on April 26, 2011.

Rolling Knolls

OUR BEST GLIMPSE of the early natural history of western Arkansas dates to 1819. The view is courtesy of botanist Thomas Nuttall from his book, *A Journal of Travels into the Arkansa Territory.*

"Nearly continuing to Mulberry creek, a fine stretch of about eight miles opens to view, affording an ample prospect of the river; its rich alluvions were now clothed in youthful verdure, and backed in the distance by bluish and empurpled hills," he wrote from a flat boat on the Arkansas River. "The beauty of the scenery was also enlivened by the melody of innumerable birds."

April 22, 1819: a high spring day in Arkansas Territory. Resident birds like Northern Cardinals and Killdeer are nesting. Big wintering flocks of Red-winged Blackbirds have broken up, with migrants headed north, but the residents with their rich *oh-kee-lah* calls are nesting in river cane and shrubbery along the river. Blue-winged Teal and Lesser Yellowlegs pour north. The sweet *oh Canada, Canada, Canada* whistles of White-throated Sparrows enliven thickets.

"The dawn of morning was again ushered in by songs of thousands of birds, re-echoing through the woods, and seeking shelter from extensive plains, which every where now border the alluvion." That was his journal entry for April 23, 1819, a day when the flatboat covered thirty-two river miles and approached the western garrison of Fort Smith.

"From hence also the prairies or grassy plains begin to be prevalent, and the trees to decrease in number and magnitude," he wrote from the confluence of Lee Creek and the Arkansas near modern Van Buren on April 24. "Contiguous to our encampment commenced a prairie seven miles in length and continuing within a mile of the garrison. The river, now presenting long and romantic views, was almost exclusively bordered with groves of cotton-woods, at this season extremely beautiful, resembling so many vistas clad in the softest and most vivid verdue, and crowded with innumerable birds . . ."

This would be a robust chorus of American Goldfinches, resplendent in their gold and black, singing as they search flowers and buds. Eastern Bluebirds, Carolina Chickadees, and the first Summer Tanagers join in. Red-shouldered Hawks occupy nests in the riparian woodlands, their *ki-yah, ki-yah* calls carrying above spring currents. Back sloughs are haunts for pairs of gorgeously attired Wood Ducks.

There is also the intriguing question about that great phantom, Ivory-billed Woodpecker. Might it also have lived in the valley of the Arkansas, its curious *tin horn* calls sounding among tall cottonwoods and giant oaks?

On April 27, Nuttall walked five miles in the vicinity of the Poteau River, "and found my labour well repaid by the discovery of several new or undescribed plants. In this direction the surface of the ground is gently broken or undulated, and thinly scattered with trees, resembling almost in this respect a cultivated park. The whole expanse of forest, hills, and dale, was now richly enameled with a profusion of beautiful and curious flowers."

His companion on many of these field trips was Dr. Russell of the Fort Smith garrison, "a gentleman, an accomplished scholar, and a sincere admirer of the simple beauties of the field of nature." Nuttall named *Monarda russeliana,* the spring horsemint, in his honor.

"On the 29th, I took an agreeable walk into the adjoining prairie, which is about two miles wide and seven long. I found it equally undulated with the surrounding woodland, and could perceive no reason for the absence of trees, except the annual conflagration . . ." or prairie burning. "Like an immense meadow, the expanse was now covered with a luxuriant herbage, and beautifully decorated with flowers, amongst which I was pleased to see Painted Cup . . ." or *Castilleja coccinea,* Indian paintbrush.

The western outpost of Nuttall's time has fantastically outgrown the two blockhouses and cabins for seventy soldiers then perched on Belle Point. Fort Smith, Van Buren, and other communities fill the huge bend and adjoining bottomlands and former prairies of the Arkansas River Valley. However, April's visitors to remnants of western Arkansas prairies can still enjoy Nuttall's Painted Cups and Dr. Russell's *Monarda.*

Remnants of curious mounds or knolls remain on open grasslands. "The numerous rounded elevations which chequer this verdant plain," Nuttall wrote, "are so many partial attempts at shrubbery and arborescent vegetation, which nature has repeatedly made, and which have only been subdued by the reiterated operation of annual burning, employed by the natives, for the purpose of hunting with more facility, and of affording a tender pasturage for the game."

Nuttall, Russell, and others traveled roughly ten miles southeast of the fort to today's Barling–Fort Chaffee area in the first two weeks of May. "Encamping near a small brook, we were favored by the usual music of frogs, and among them heard a species which almost exactly imitated the lowing of a calf. Just as night commenced, the cheerless howling of a distant wolf accosted our ears amidst the tranquil solitude, and the whole night we were serenaded with the vociferations of the two species of whip-poor-will."

Now, please return Nuttall to the bookshelf and join me in the 1950s. I'm an elementary kid in Fort Smith. I live on the old rolling knolls of Nuttall's acquaintance, though I don't know them as prairie. Grass is grass: what I know is ball fields and mowing our yard.

The eighty grassy acres of Rolling Knolls Country Club in Fort Smith occupied what to me as a kid seemed a limitless sea of small, generally symmetrical mounds (knolls). I didn't know it back then, but wherever found in western Arkansas, the knolls tend to be somewhat regularly spaced, have a rough uniformity in height (often four to six feet), and are somewhat circular in outline. Rolling Knolls was on what was in my youth the edge of Fort Smith, adjacent my Kennedy grandparents' home. Their shiplap-sided house, with big garden and chickens, was a lot like the farmhouse they left in Logan County, near Magazine, an area also covered by "rolling knolls."

Since Nuttall's time, the once extensive prairies of western Arkansas have been plowed for crops and now converted to neighborhoods like the one where I grew up. Rolling knolls were bulldozed flat to build our post–World War II subdivision, Sunnymeade. Most rolling knolls in western Arkansas have been similarly flattened.

In the early 1960s, James Quinn from the University of Arkansas–Fayetteville described them as follows: "Mounds range from 20–60

Remnant prairie mounds, shallow pool from an early spring rain, and large hardwood trees. Agri Park at Agricultural Experiment Station, University of Arkansas, Fayetteville.

feet in diameter and from 2–8 feet high. They are slightly asymmetrical, somewhat elongated and steepened on the leeward side. All are similarly oriented. The pattern of distribution is random in northwest Arkansas. The most abundant mounds, those composed completely of eolian windblown material, occupy flat or level surfaces."

Among ecologists there is general agreement on a "hypsothermal" period roughly two to six thousand years before present. Compared to today, during the hypsothermal, the climate was hotter with less rainfall. The hypsothermal caused eastern forests to contract and prairies typical of the Great Plains to advance into western Arkansas. Windblown soil might have collected around deeply rooted bushes, eventually forming mounds. Other researchers think that mounds resulted from excavations and soil movement associated with colonies of pocket gophers.

You can see the process right now in places like Chesney Prairie Natural Area in Benton County. Pocket gophers, coyotes, terrestrial crayfish, and other creatures there continuously excavate or otherwise disturb the soil.

Noticing the debate, some snarky people throw in yet another theory: Sioux Indians made them so they'd have a good dry place to pitch their teepees. It's something fun to talk about on a field trip.

Over the years I have watched mounds that cover fifty acres on the University Experiment Farm in Fayetteville. During heavy rains, water collects and stands in the saucer-like depressions between mounds. Eastern Meadowlarks perch atop them, in the relative dry. Killdeer, Wilson's Snipe, and American Golden-Plovers probe for insects in the shallows. I haven't noticed any Sioux teepees though.

Benton County, home base of the burgeoning Walmart empire, is roughly seventy-five miles north of Thomas Nuttall country. Higher, drier fields with mounds—leveled long ago for row crops—now host Walmart Supercenters and rapidly growing towns like Springdale, Rogers, and Bentonville. Here and there are small patches of big bluestem grass. Like pages from a history book, Indian grass clings along fencerows and railroad rights-of-way.

The combinations of prairie conditions—open grassland, mounds, both upland and low lying fields, and thickets of trees and shrubs—have long provided special habitats for birds. Yellow-crowned Night-Herons forage for the terrestrial crawfish associated with open wet fields. Here too, American Woodcocks perform their early spring dances. The lowest and wettest areas retain more water—habitat for migrating Blue-winged Teal. Thickets of low bushes and tall grass in wet areas are suitable for Common Yellowthroats.

Bell's Vireo nests in wet thickets composed of rough-leafed dogwood and indigo bush. Bell's Vireo was once common in such habitat in the Ozarks of northwest Arkansas. They have become unusual as the habitat has been degraded, drained, and bulldozed into oblivion. Willow Flycatchers once nested in wet thickets in Benton County. This population disappeared after construction of a factory complex. A few Bell's Vireos remain at Baker Prairie Natural Area in Harrison, but this population is also under intense development pressure.

When we think of the Ozarks, we think almost exclusively of mountains and forests. The prevalence of former prairies in western Arkansas probably comes as a surprise. In a collective sense, we have forgotten that wild bison grazed here, that Greater Prairie-Chickens once danced here. We've forgotten that the common grass here was big bluestem, not fescue. We suffer a dangerous amnesia about our origins. It's dangerous because if we don't understand where we've come from, we are just as likely clueless about where we are heading. Societies that hope to endure cannot afford such amnesia.

During his trip through western Arkansas in 1819, Thomas Nuttall walked over much of what would be called the Massard Prairie at Fort Smith—likely including the Rolling Knolls of my youth—as well as the Cedar Prairie a little south, including Fort Chaffee. "We kept westwardly, toward the bank of the Pottoe," he wrote on May 16, 1819, "and found the whole country a prairie, full of luxuriant grass about knee high, in which we surprised herds of fleeing deer . . ." They killed two bears feeding in the prairies on May 17. They discovered bison in the prairie within a few days.

Another 1819 visitor to western Arkansas, Frank Pierce, came up the White River, visiting the site that would become Fayetteville. While here, he saw a herd of bison grazing in the low, wet prairie that forms the modern day industrial park in south Fayetteville. The central part of Fayetteville, Prairie Township, was clothed in native prairie grass. Where today stands a town square with brick buildings, lovely gardens, and ornamental trees, there were Greater Prairie-Chickens, Dickcissels, Grasshopper Sparrows, and Eastern Kingbirds.

Here the amnesia is total. The Fayetteville city administration building sits right in the middle of Prairie Township, but you'd be hard pressed to find anyone there, or anyone around the lovely town square, who could explain why they're standing in Prairie Township, rather than, say, Razorback Township.

In 1857–1858, the paleobotanist Leo Lesquereux authored part of a report on western Arkansas. In reference to counties near the Arkansas River, he wrote "Most of the too extensive flat lands . . . are prairies, which, underlain as they are by impermeable beds of shales or of fine clay, are generally marshy . . . A great part of Sebastian and the south of Franklin County is occupied by prairies underlain by clay and shales, and still mostly uncultivated . . . They are too wet, too hard, too clayey, say the farmers, who clear land in forests surrounding the prairies . . ."

These old Cherokee Prairies may have once occupied as much

Brewer's Blackbirds following bison during the annual Christmas Bird Count at Tallgrass Prairie Preserve in northeastern Oklahoma on January 4, 2011.

as 135,000 acres in the western portion of the Arkansas River Valley. Something over 1000 acres have been preserved in Franklin County. Henslow's Sparrows have been found there during the nesting season.

Leo Lesquereux visited the Osage Prairie, originally roughly ten miles east-west and two to three miles north-south in Benton County. Modern Rogers and Bentonville, including the Walmart empire, are built on the Osage. Lesquereux wrote, "the far-extended and beautiful prairies of the Osages . . . are flat and of wide extent, and the lowest parts of the surface are marshy and somewhat difficult to drain . . . In the spring the low grounds are covered by three feet of water. Where drainage has been attended to, the prairie soil produces, on average, forty bushels of corn, or fifteen to twenty bushels of wheat an acre, or one thousand to fifteen hundred pounds of tobacco. It gives also fine crops of oats and of hay. Benton, the county seat, is beautifully situated in the middle of these fertile prairies . . ." An eight-acre fragment of the Osage Prairie, Searles Prairie Natural Area, is preserved near the Walmart world headquarters in Bentonville.

Now time has largely erased the Kennedy place on what is now North 30th Street in Fort Smith. Rolling Knolls Country Club is gone, mounds leveled, grassland covered by homes. As to our origins, the amnesia is near universal.

Centerton is pivotal in some respects to the unfolding tale of western Arkansas. It lies within the boundaries of the former Osage Prairie in Benton County. The town has its origins in the 1830s, when a pioneer family headed by James McKissick settled on lands dominated by an impressive artesian spring. A village sprung up associated with railroad construction in 1900.

Benton County was once most famous for clear artesian flows gushing from numerous caves and cave-like openings. Siloam Springs, Springtown, Eldorado Springs, Sulphur Springs, Chalybeate Spring, Bluff Spring, Osage Spring, Cave Spring, Electric Spring—and directly relevant to our purpose, McKissick Spring—are all Benton County place names.

When I first saw it thirty years ago, Centerton was a remote community of two hundred. It was open, undeveloped, a relatively treeless grassland. It was like visiting Kansas. I think Nuttall would have recognized it. That was before Walmart, with its headquarters only four miles east in Bentonville, had its first billion dollar year (1979).

The presence of so many natural springs in Benton County was considered, well, a "natural" marvel. The Walmart phenomenon is our contemporary marvel. I don't think Nuttall would recognize it now.

The thirty-mile drive from Fayetteville then required at least forty-five minutes on Arkansas 112. The road zigzagged along the edges of pastures and hayfields, turning at sharp angles while following pioneer property lines. It crossed two streams on one-lane bridges. It connected other small communities including Tontitown, Elm Springs, and Cave Springs. Farmers rather than Walmart eighteen-wheelers set the speed limits. You gave way to farmers hauling hay and heavy trucks with chicken feed.

It didn't pay to hurry. There was no need to, really—the country along 112 was full of Dickcissels and Eastern Kingbirds. Loggerhead Shrikes were common. It felt expansive, like Kansas.

Nevertheless, we had days when we couldn't go fast enough. I'm talking about spring migration's peak in western Arkansas, mid-April to mid-May. Birds fly on warm air masses as they move north from their southern wintering range. A cold air mass stops them. When the fronts collide, they cease migrating and "fall out." Birders, too, fall out—from family, jobs, and school—to look for migrants.

Fall-outs are days to head for the shoreline-like mudflats at Centerton. There could be fifteen to twenty species of shorebirds—golden-plovers, godwits, phalaropes, and yellowlegs. There could be a big flock of Franklin's Gulls. It's a good day to hit wet bottomland fields along the Arkansas River at Van Buren, crop fields at Moffett just west of Fort Smith, big shallow farm ponds with broad muddy edges at Waldron in Scott County on Nuttall's old "Pottoe" prairie. That's what our hurry is about. Migration doesn't wait for anyone.

As they say in shopper's paradise, "You snooze you lose." Same goes for birding.

The far eastern edge of the Great Plains butts into the forests of western Arkansas. Shorebirds that nest in Canada and Alaska use this edge. In the eons before the hatchery or big wet crop fields, migrants stopped in temporary or seasonal wetlands where they fed on soft-bodied prey, and rested on the edges of natural shallow pools. Soras and Marsh Wrens can still be common in these wet grassy edges. In rainy weather—the best birding days—many small, insect-rich pools form in the shallows between rolling knolls.

At the state fish hatchery, ponds are drained to facilitate catching fish. As the water is drained, mudflats appear, mimicking natural conditions. Blue-winged Teal and waders like Green Herons and Great Egrets hunt the shallows. Migrating terns and raptors like Ospreys forage over ponds. Peregrine Falcons chase shorebirds.

Until recent years, the hatchery was virtually surrounded by low-lying former prairie fields, many with mounds. Water stood in them, too, especially between mounds. A trip to the hatchery included scanning these wet, mounded fields, which provided additional suitable habitat.

Franklin's Gulls and Forster's Terns make a brief migratory stopover in a flooded field near Chesney Prairie Natural Area on April 24, 2011.

On a given day in late April and early May, shorebird stopovers at Centerton include Semipalmated Plover, Killdeer, Lesser Yellowlegs, Wilson's Phalarope, plus numerous species with sandpiper in their names: Spotted, Semipalmated, Least, White-rumped, Baird's, Pectoral. A few of another ten species also pour through. We are always thrilled to see Hudsonian Godwits.

Spring migration is concentrated over a short period, as compared to fall, which is spread out from early July into October. A good fall day at Centerton includes Semipalmated Plover, Killdeer, Greater and Lesser Yellowlegs, Wilson's Snipe, and sandpipers including Solitary, Spotted, Upland, Semipalmated, Western, Least, Pectoral, Stilt, Buff-breasted. By early October, add Dunlin and Long-billed Dowitcher.

So that's what the hurry to Centerton is about. That's why birders are out with their scopes along the Arkansas River and in the Moffett bottoms west of Fort Smith. We want to see the birds. But there's no denying that big landscape changes are continuing.

Most of the natural prairie wetlands seen by Nuttall and Lesquereux disappeared early. Wet soils weren't conducive to one of the prairie settler's earliest sources of income: wheat, and later, apples, chickens, and cattle. Prairie mounds were plowed, and wet prairies drained. More recently, the prairie disappeared under waves of conversion from native grasses like big bluestem to introduced species like fescue.

This has occurred as a backdrop to Walmart's first billion-dollar week in 1993. Burgeoning retirement developments centered at Bella Vista lie just north of the hatchery. Walmart world headquarters is east in Bentonville. Northwest Arkansas Regional Airport, a bare few miles southwest, sits upon once high-quality prairie habitat. Discerning travelers arriving and departing the airport may hear singing by prairie Horned Larks and Grasshopper Sparrows, now relegated to isolated patches of suitable habitat posted with "For Sale" signs and no doubt soon to disappear entirely.

These developments are changing Centerton and its hatchery. The once relatively quiet, open prairie is filling up with homes and businesses. Housing developments steadily march toward the hatchery. "For Sale" signs are visible behind flocks of migrating Wilson's Snipe. It no longer seems like rural Kansas.

From two hundred residents twenty-five years ago, Centerton is now five thousand and adding daily. Hatchery visitors see 737s overhead more often than large birds of prey, like Ospreys. A look into the big sky of the old Osage Prairie is likely to bring into focus, not a desired flock of migrating Franklin's Gulls, but rather a web of jet trails. We hear booms, too, but not those of nesting season Greater Prairie-Chickens. Who shall we blame for this, other than ourselves?

I'm thinking Joe Woolbright is a latter day Thomas Nuttall. He does not suffer from amnesia about the importance of prairies in understanding western Arkansas.

We are out on Chesney Prairie Natural Area, near Joe's hometown, Siloam Springs. He is the fourth generation of his family to live on the former prairies in Benton County. His mother grew up on Chesney. Considering Joe's children and grandchildren, his family has lived here for six generations.

During his 1819 Arkansas visit, Nuttall wrote about "the annual conflagration" of fire that kept the prairie clear of brush and encouraged the native grasses and flowers. Here I am today with a modern *"conflageur"* himself—if you don't mind my coining the term—Chesney's

July 12, 2007: Joe Woolbright of Siloam Springs stands in prairie sod cut and moved from Stump Prairie as a result of the widening of Highway 59. Under his direction, the sod was successfully replanted at Chesney Prairie Natural Area as part of restoration efforts there.

Contract Land Steward, Mr. Woolbright. He burns the prairie to achieve the same conditions noted by Nuttall.

The Arkansas Department of Natural Heritage conferred Joe's title. He is also steward of the few additional acres of native prairie remaining elsewhere in northwest Arkansas. These jobs are his passion, but his income is mainly from Woolbright Electric, founded by his father, and now including a third generation, Joe's son and extended family.

Chesney contains almost all of what remains of the pioneer era Lindsley Prairie once covering twenty-four square miles. It has disappeared under the growing city of Siloam Springs, pastures, cattle herds, and the world's most impressive poultry concentration. Joe Woolbright is grand champion of what remains of Lindsley Prairie. And he intends to bring as much of it back as possible. He founded Ozark Ecological

Restoration, Incorporated to push forward his agenda of natural habitat restoration.

I'm at Chesney Prairie in May trying to keep up with Joe as he searches for and greets his old friends, the native orchids. By "trying to keep up," I mean I'm attempting to absorb the common and scientific names that leap from his active mind like welder's sparks. I'm in luck. *Platanthera lacea* and *Calopogon oklahomensis* are blooming. Joe also provides the common names: ragged fringed orchid and Oklahoma grass pink orchid.

The *Platanthera* is striking because of its upright spike and the long flower fringes. We're in full-blown admiration when Joe's cell phone summons his attention. He has a construction crew wiring a big house in Gravette. Problem 1: a carpenter hasn't shown up for work. Problem 2: someone must leave the Gravette job to meet a contractor at Decatur. Joe is on the phone about two minutes and says he will handle it. He then tries to reach his son Alex.

The *Calopogon* is most interesting because Chesney is one of just a few places it occurs in Arkansas. I want to take a few photographs, but it's a blinding sunny day. No problem: the Contract Land Steward takes off his shirt and shades the plant. Then the phone sings again. Joe owns a trailer park. Its residents are mostly Mexican immigrants, the working backbone of our burgeoning poultry industry. The caller is interested in an empty trailer. Another couple of minutes pass and then Joe seamlessly segues to orchids like his mind was never away. It's all in a day's work.

I compliment Joe on his multi-tasking, noting that he seems to know a lot about very disparate realities. I'm thinking about the divide between *Platanthera* say, and the trailer park. With no hesitation and no forethought, he responds like a veteran melodramatist: "He knows a lot, but a lot of what he knows ain't so."

In his sixties, Joe is energetic, muscular, operates with a quick smile and quick scorn for hypocrisy, including his own. He sports liberalism midst a conservative community. He was an early member of the Sierra Club in Arkansas. He serves on the board of directors of the Ozark Natural Science Center, helping bridge a wide divide in a conservative region. Christian fundamentalists send their children to ONSC summer camps, often taught by biologists not trained in Biblical "creation science."

Call him a radical—he will appreciate you for it. He relishes political discussion with the conservative farmers and businessmen with whom he grew up and still cordially meets in the early morning coffee shop. Like them, he is a businessman, but he does not mark down his wide-ranging opinions on the affairs of the day in order to make them palatable over sausage and scrambled eggs.

His prairie management is run out of his company, Ozark Ecological Restoration, but the mainspring of his business operations is Woolbright Electric. Among his clients are big poultry companies, the Cherokee casinos just over the state line in Oklahoma, and area banks. In short, this environmental activist rubs elbows and his ideas with the rich and powerful of northwest Arkansas. He's even taken some of them out to hear *Gryllotalpas major*, the prairie mole cricket. The males sing—or perhaps I should say stridulate—for females. They occur only on the unplowed prairie, so just like the orchids, these crickets provide a way to assess ecosystem health.

The stridulations are to the human ear a seemingly endless series of *ur-ur-ur-urs*. No doubt, it's attractive to cricket females and the chorus enlivens the old prairie. I set up a recording and collect forty minutes of crickets and burn it to a CD. This I present to Joe in a ceremony marked by "mellerdramer," the corrupted melodramatic form marked by considerable buffoonery. He's quite pleased by the spirit of it all, and tells me that he now plays it regularly in his wife Jackie's Suburban. "Most people start reacting badly at about two minutes," he notes, laconically, "and by five minutes they are complaining of torture."

Joe's fertile mind hatches a new business: sell it to the Department of Defense. Instead of siccing dogs on detainees in the War on Terrorism, they could just subject them to incessant prairie mole cricket stridulations. It's a whole new frontier in national defense, and he expects the Pentagon to go for it. He could then retire from all business, except prairie restoration. For this, and other out-of-the-box speculations, Joe has been crowned "Walking Eagle" because, as he himself notes, he's so full of shit he can't fly. But that's all for show. There's something dead serious going on behind the humor.

No problem is more vexing for a Land Steward than alien plants. Western Arkansas's prairies were virtually limitless in Nuttall's time and remained so through the first few generations of Joe's family at Siloam

Rattlesnake master with numerous insect pollinators at Chesney Prairie Natural Area on July 10, 2011.

Springs. The concept—not to mention the reality—of non-native plants lay far in the future. By the time Joe came along, isolated, postage stamp–size prairie patches were completely surrounded in northwest Arkansas by an alien landscape smothered by non-native plants.

These plants invade the unplowed prairie and overwhelm the once common and widespread natives—like orchids. Protecting and restoring the prairie is a battle, or actually a war. Joe has, as the Bible says, "girded up his loins." With his strong hands and back, he's ready to meet the invader. He is constantly bending down to pull out by its roots the alien invasive *Barbarea vulgaris,* yellow rocket.

But the war involves more than yanking up *Barbarea.* Here is the businessman and property owner in his boots, blue jeans and T-shirt, ten-gallon sprayer in his hands. Now, instead of *Calopogon oklahomensis,* he stops to discuss the merits of herbicides like Glyphosate, Immazapyr, and Triclopry. He tries various mixes and strengths on experimental patches. The idea is to regain ground for natives.

At Baker Prairie near Harrison, he's at war with a patch of sericea

Male Scissor-tailed Flycatcher, now a familiar summer resident in the former prairies of western Arkansas. Photographed in Prairie Township near Hindsville in May 2005.

lespedeza. At Chesney he's attacking a highly aggressive alien, *Holcus lanatus,* velvet grass, which has virtually excluded native plants from seasonal wetlands. Midst warfare, he's mindful that the velvet grass battlefield is home to several rare native sedges. These must be protected as he destroys the velvet grass.

His cell sounds again. As he talks, I'm watching a thick patch of *Helianthus mollis,* ashy sunflowers, a widespread native characteristic of our prairies. They are common at Chesney and so are the American Goldfinches seeking their numerous seeds. As spring turns to summer, these sunflowers ripen and goldfinches have an abundant supply of seeds and insects as they begin to nest.

Woolbright Electric still pays most bills, but this latter day Nuttall is also paid in orchids and big bluestem grass. He's laid the spray on velvet grass so that the native Indian grass will again flourish. Then, with today's battle done, he's ready for a beer, laughs, and any anti-environmental Republicans not yet vanquished at the country club.

Prairie-Chickens rose up in great flocks before pioneers, but these birds were shot and their habitat plowed into oblivion long before our time. We cannot unplow the rolling knolls. That is, we cannot undo our history. But are we eternally condemned to amnesia about what's important? Can we not learn something from our past—see what there is of value in our past and consider what we might choose to change today?

A modern visitor to western Arkansas may find that Bell's Vireos have commenced nesting in wet thickets, at least in the Fort Smith area. Northern Bobwhites are whistling across open grasslands. Eastern Meadowlark singing fills the air, eggs in their first nests are carefully hidden below the developing grass.

"The dawn of a cloudy day, after to us a wakeful night, was ushered in by the melodious chorus of many thousands of birds, agreeably dispersing the solemnity of the ambiguous twilight," Nuttall wrote.

The gift in understanding the losses in our natural history is that after so many decades of determined neglect and destruction, we are now growing in our appreciation of these grassy expanses. We nurture our spirits in this process.

Between Rock, a hand-colored etching by Richard Stauffacher, 1998.

Richard

A SHALLOW FARM pond of irregular shape is the main distinguishing feature of a vast weedy field. This is a farm well past its glory days. There are scattered post oaks, a collapsed shed, and broken-down fences. Low conical mounds mark a former prairie. The pond must once have had as its official business cows and horses, and maybe farm kids. Today it hosts the occasional flock of migrating Double-crested Cormorants, a few American White Pelicans, and sparrows, ducks, geese, and whatnot. That's unofficial business. I'll bet Wild Turkeys and bobwhite quail coveys know this spot, too.

Most of these are birds that nest well to the north of Arkansas, all across the great north country of Alaska, Canada, the northern United States. During their western Arkansas stopover, they tank up on insects and fish, and then continue on—south to the Gulf of Mexico and South America, or in the other season, north. Some of them know this pond, in a big field, under an even bigger sky.

On my wall hangs a hand-tinted etching, *Savannah Sparrows* by Richard Stauffacher of Fayetteville. That's why I'm thinking now about that weedy field with its generous pond and welcoming sky. The striped and streaked patterns of brown, yellow, black, and buff-white on the two small birds blend with the weedy stalks and leaves of smartweed. This is an aquatic plant that grows profusely in the pond shallows.

Savannah Sparrows are as typical of the old prairie grasslands as were the nineteenth-century herds of bison. Two birds perch expectantly on twisted stalks in Richard's etching. It's an intimate look, since the birds are deep in the vegetation, well hidden from view. Well, not from everyone's view.

Over the years, Richard's etchings have captured a host of creatures and natural environments of western Arkansas. Just a few examples:

nesting Great Blue Herons on the Illinois River in early spring and maidenhair ferns dripping over lichen-encrusted sandstones. He etched a small flock of White-throated Sparrows and Dark-eyed Juncos in the snow. More subjects: Northern Bobwhites in another old field, flocks of ducklike American Coots among lotus pads at Lake Fayetteville, a single dog-day cicada on the bark of an oak tree.

He's also been inspired by the wildflowers that arise, Lazarus-like, each spring from the forest floor: jack-in-the-pulpit, trout lily, and the majestic unfurling of hickory buds. And the massive bluffs rising above the Buffalo River.

There is an old joke about the artist who lures a young woman to his room by promising to show her his etchings. The joke may date all the way back to the sixteenth century or even further, when artists discovered that an image could be etched into a metal plate using acids. It was interesting then, and now.

Once the image is etched, thick ink is smeared on the plate and then wiped off. Ink remains within the etched portions. The plate is pressed firmly onto paper. Several plates and different types of ink may be used to create complex images. Printed etchings can be hand colored in a variety of ways, using paints and pencils.

Of course, why go to all the trouble? Why not just take a digital picture and be done with it? Good question. A typical camera image reflects what has been viewed, and little else. The handmade image is a one-of-a-kind impression. It bears witness to the artist.

For an artist to make a living, it must be sold for a high price. That's fine if the artwork achieves the fame of Van Gogh, but even Van Goghs had little commercial value during the life of that artist. On the other hand, what if that impression could be produced in a small edition, say one to three hundred copies? Since each was printed, colored, and numbered, each would be the unique work of the artist. Each print could be sold for a modest price. Fine art then becomes available to the many, rather than just the few.

Back in the mid-1980s, Richard sold hand-colored pen and ink drawings at Fayetteville's Farmer's Market. One of these was an image approximately five by seven inches featuring a silver-spotted skipper perched on a rose vervain. While impressionistic in rendering, the spe-

Savannah Sparrows, a hand-colored etching by Richard Stauffacher, 1982.

cies was identifiable. Skippers are among our commonest butterflies; the vervain does well just about anywhere there's sunlight. There's beauty in life's commonplace realities.

This picture features a disciplined attention to detail. It projects a sense of landscape enlivened by the unique and the particular. I have wondered about the sources of this quality. Richard does not hold a degree in biology, but biologists are enthusiastic about his work. The spirit promoting this style has something to do with his growing up.

If you visit his home in Fayetteville, you will note a dog, a cat, a bluebird house, fruit trees, vegetable garden, several sheds, an old van. In other words, typically and comfortably Arkansas. But he did not grow up here. He was born in Russellville in 1948, but almost immediately his family returned to Africa. He grew up among Africans, missionaries, and a wild fauna and flora most of us know only from documentaries broadcast on Arkansas Educational Television Network.

His parents, Gladys and Claudon Stauffacher, were missionaries.

Claudon was born in Kenya in 1910 at Rumuruti, among the Masai, where his parents were missionaries. His father came to Kenya in 1903 and married Richard's grandmother there in 1906. Claudon returned as a missionary in 1933. He and Gladys were married in Kenya in 1942.

From shortly after Richard's birth until 1960, the family pursued their calling as ministers and social workers in the old Belgian Congo, leaving there only because of chaos accompanying independence. The Stauffachers then moved to Kenya when Richard was sixteen. While kids in the United States were growing up with Elvis, the Beatles, and Mickey Mantle, Richard was growing with the Masai people of Kenya's highlands, with elephants and leopards, zebras, impalas. Richard's mother chronicled the family's life and work in *Faster Beats the Drum* (168 pages, African Inland Mission, Pearl River, NY 1978).

Because his parent's work was remote, Richard was educated in boarding schools in the Congo and Kenya. He found his own balance in a vast landscape. He took a correspondence course in taxidermy, shot birds and other small animals, stuffed and preserved them. These are typically pursuits of a scientist in the making, a modern-day Audubon, or at least an active mind concerned with nature's particulars. He learned anatomy, color, and form at firsthand. He learned to work by himself, to be creative in an environment that would have been insufferably lonely for people with a more regular growing up.

Richard returned to the United States in 1965. After service in the navy, he earned his BS in fine art from John Brown University in Siloam Springs (1975). He began producing work like the skipper and vervain pen-and-ink, but it was apparent that it would be hard to sell enough of them at five to ten dollars a piece to make a living.

How many of you readers remember the woman who played violin in the Northwest Arkansas Symphony—and for flowers on the Fayetteville Square? Just think back to the early 1980s, when the Square was struggling. Its heyday was the 1920s. By the 1970s, it was like an abandoned field, full of tumbled-down bricks, and struggling in what then seemed a hopeless struggle against shiny malls. The woman earned some of her living playing her violin for flowers planted as an attraction, to lure and to comfort shoppers. She played in those years when old Fayetteville was rapidly changing into something different.

Then, as now, the flowers represented something of hope. We learned only later that she was sick during the last year of her work on the Square.

Do you remember the boy with her on those strolls? That woman, who called herself Free (changing her name from Lenore Mark), died when her son Isaac was eight. Before her passing, she had the presence of mind to entrust the rearing of her son to a friend who did not have children of his own. He befriended the boy, taking him hiking in the National Forest at Wedington while his mother played in the symphony, and continued while she struggled for life against the cancer that slowly claimed her life. The man was Richard Stauffacher.

Besides selling his drawings on the Square, Richard was framing art for Wendell Cullers at the Art Emporium on Block Street and for Jay Emerson at the Frame Place on Dickson. During this time he met several people who would have a tremendous influence on his development. Printmaker Ed Bernstein, then in the U of A–Fayetteville Art Department, allowed Richard use of his studio and equipment. Another influence was Susan Raymond.

Susan, who at this time was a regular at the War Eagle Arts and Crafts Fair, owned a small, professional-quality etching press that she used to produce limited editions of her Ozarks country–inspired drawings. She owned a farm in Madison County. Richard made a trip out there to learn how the press worked. She also handed him a catalog from Graphic Chemical and Ink in Chicago, the standard supplier for etching supplies. The rest, as they say, is history.

Richard went from the one-of-a-kind drawings like the skipper and vervain to editions turned out on Susan's press. One of these early etchings featured a small and seemingly obscure butterfly among dead leaves and twigs on the forest floor. While the etching measures only approximately four by five inches, it encompasses a landscape enlivened by particulars, attractively organized in a small space.

In this milieu of frame shops and working artists, Richard's work was introduced to Ria Foster of Island International Artists, based on Guemes Island in northern Puget Sound, Washington. Foster and her representatives travel to galleries all over the country with an artist's work.

Seeing Richard's potential, Foster helped Richard buy a large press so that he could move up from the compact format of Susan's press. With more potential to make a living, Richard expanded his production.

In 1986, Richard and Isaac moved from Fayetteville to Guemes Island where he assumed the role of master printer for Ria's Black Raven Press. He made a steady living, and Isaac grew up. But beautiful as it was on an island in Puget Sound, it was never home. In 1993, he and Isaac returned, this time not to an apartment, but a house on a few acres in the Mount Comfort area of Fayetteville. They bought the property with Susan Raymond, her partner Liz Lester, and their daughter Gale.

Ria Foster works with many artists who, like Richard, have learned to draw, but who, unlike Richard, lack technical skills in etching and printing. Ria saw in Richard not only the work of an artist with a love of nature, but a highly skilled craftsman converting interesting ideas into technically accomplished etchings. After Richard returned to Fayetteville in 1993, she shipped drawings by other artists so Richard could make the plates. She also repeatedly shipped him back to Guemes to work with the artists themselves during a series of workshops.

Richard and Martha Whelan were married in 1999. Martha is a hospice nurse whose compassionate professionalism has carried her into the lives of folks all over northwest Arkansas. Besides a flourishing vegetable garden and fruit trees, Richard and Martha share a practical hobby and attractive living yard art: chickens. They walk the yard, inspect the garden, and generally keep the place in order.

Richard has gotten into Ozark rocks with big format etchings. You've been to bluff lines like these if you've hiked in the Ozarks. He's finding spots where the old multilayered rock strata have been eroding for hundreds of millions of years. It's too rough for commercial development. Unfettered nature has been allowed to take her course. Grapevines, fence lizards, and small secretive snakes have run of the place. Cavelike rock overhangs may once have sheltered Native Americans from a snowstorm. Deer and bears pass through this country.

If you are out there in late March, you can just about bet there will be Black-and-white Warblers there, fresh from the Neotropics. You can also bet Blue-gray Gnatcatchers will be nearby in the old cedars. Even with its frenetic pace of growth, the Fayetteville area is still blessed with such places: it could be Lake Wilson Park, or atop Washington Mountain

Richard and Martha Stauffacher in 2000.

in Finger Park. It could be on the long rocky ridge in the Ozark National Forest at Wedington. Many such places grace the Buffalo River country.

In his etching *Rocks in Spring,* lichens are silver-gray; moss, emerald green; massive sandstone outcrops, worn and rounded. The rich tangle of trees and vines is essentially leafless. Rooted in thin soils atop the rocks is a single serviceberry (or sarvis) tree, small and generally overlooked in an understory among better known trees, the dogwoods and redbuds. It must be March, perhaps middle of the month, because the serviceberry has burst into a snowstorm of delicate white blossoms, enlivening a winter background of gray. Serviceberries bloom well ahead of redbuds and dogwoods.

Richard's *Rocks in Spring* contains many more details when compared to his pieces from the 1980s. We easily share his interest in this otherwise nondescript tree that now, in March, so dominates the landscape. Technically speaking, the etching's format is large at twelve by eighteen inches. The lines are complex, rich, varied, and layered. The hand coloring is refined, elegant, and delicate. Taken in the whole, *Rocks in Spring* fetches the viewer out for a last visit with winter, a first commune with spring.

The most striking of the birds that nest here are Great Blue Herons. You've seen them out there along the river where they fish for frogs and minnows. I'm thinking about this while looking at Richard's etching *Great Blue Heron.* A solitary bird stands along the water's edge. The background is an expansive open country horizon, with masses of sedges along the water's edge. The alert bird dominates psychological space—a giant in the landscape, cameo of ancient reality.

This is the bird seen as we hurry to work and struggle to be on time—at a farm pond, in the far field, along the highway. It's at a distance from our car windows, without binoculars—before the bird flies into its ancient space. It's a figure in the landscape we presumably dominate.

Another etching, *Heronry,* encompasses the nesting season's onset. Leafless upper boughs of sycamores arch and twine into an early sky. Above, a single Great Blue Heron—could be that bird we saw as we were rushing up the highway—approaches the creek bottom with wings set and neck curled, gliding toward stick masses that seem rearrangements of an old sycamore's upper boughs. Down among the upper twigs and branches are the stick masses themselves, attended by other birds.

There could be a future generation of herons in the making there. It could be our vital connection with time in the far, far future. We could stop for a while and try to figure this out, but we have our own livings to make—our own versions of small fish and tadpoles to catch, our own young to rear.

Heronry seems relatively simple. Taken in one way, this etching of herons nesting may be construed as an impressionistic image of nature's annual cycle, and nothing more. The biology is covered. Underneath there's an essential theme. The grove of trees is fishing the sky.

Several decades of etching have passed. We have moved from the 1970s to the new millennium. I get the distinct impression that my friend Richard is headed back to his roots. I don't mean he's moving back to Africa. Rather, he is re-creating Africa in Fayetteville. It turns out Africa has always been there. It's just been waiting to express itself.

Africa is sprouting up all over his studio and the three acres he shares with Martha. On his website, Richard refers to this as "the Africa connection." Boy, it's really getting connected. For example, Richard has recently taken a Swahili class at U of A–Fayetteville. Swahili is the trade language for central and east coast countries like Kenya, Uganda, and Tanzania. Richard spoke it as a kid.

He has been almost completely focused on themes local to the

"Sunlit Sagebrush," a hand-colored etching by Richard Stauffacher, 2001.

Ozarks in western Arkansas for most of the years I've known him. Early on there were a few hints of his roots in Africa. Now I'm noticing a strong flow of Africa coming out of his studio.

My first hint came from an early etching (1986). It was not a bluff scene or flowering serviceberries. Richard set *Two Trees* within a savannah in Kenya's Kedong Valley. Richard's father and other missionaries used to camp in the valley. *Two Trees* has now been joined by etchings of a fine old Cape buffalo, an elephant, and zebras. The elephant etching *In Some Brush* was juried into a fall 2010 show featuring artists of northwest Arkansas at the Arts Center of the Ozarks.

The Africa connection is not just etchings. Kenyan George Ndiritu is a slime mold specialist. He and Richard hiked the Ozarks when George had time away from his dissertation research at U of A–Fayetteville. After finishing his PhD, George returned to research and education for the National Museums of Kenya.

One day while I was visiting the studio, another Kenyan, Antony Ndugo, stopped by. Antony works for Tyson Foods. He has made a vegetable garden near Richard's studio. Corn, collards, and beans growing there would be familiar to all Kenyans.

George Ndiritu and Richard Stauffacher on the hawksbill in the Upper Buffalo Wilderness in Newton County, Arkansas, in July 2007. During the hike, George shared his interest and expertise in slime molds.

As soon as he entered the room, Antony and Richard engaged in a brief conversation in Swahili. Richard spoke the Congo version, which is called Kingwana, as a kid. It's back, here in the Ozarks.

The big pieces of life's ecological puzzle, like Bald Eagles and Ring-billed Gulls, are fairly easy to see. Many of the smaller pieces are harder and they tend to get buried as time moves on. Invariably, we miss their potential richness. Whether we are aware of it or not, these are moments in our lives, moments from the stream of our times.

Headed back to his roots, Richard is reclaiming a life he knew a half century ago. It is combined now with a rich body of work celebrating the western Ozarks.

God's Second Bible

"It may be seen standing motionless, in lonely dignity, on some far distant point that breaks the shoreline . . . its stately figure looms up in the distance, as with graceful, stealthy tread it wades along in search of its prey. Perhaps you have seen it from afar and think you can gain a closer intimacy, but its eyes and ears are keener than yours . . . even as it takes its departure, you will stand and admire the slow and dignified strokes of its great, black-tipped wing"

–Arthur Cleveland Bent,
Life Histories of North American Marsh Birds

I DRIVE, SHOP at malls, enjoy sports, and sometimes go to church. However, I rarely connect with any of this in a spiritual way. I am filled with awe and wonder by a flight of Hudsonian Godwits over seasonally wet grasslands in western Arkansas. For these and like things, I give praise and thanks. I offer my silent prayers that the negative works of humans will not be the end of these manifestations.

If pressed, and on a day when I feel cranky, I will tell friends and associates that they better get their religion walking in the woods or floating the Buffalo River. I fear that if I'm not in the field with binoculars and a bird book, I could be damned for the sin of ignoring what God created.

Considering the above, I can see how some folks might jump to the conclusion that when I go birding on a Sunday, it's a species of heathenish worship, a corruption of my heritage as a Southern Baptist. The logical assumption is that we who grew up as believers must, come Sunday morning, find a pew, or something like a pew, to honor the Creator, like I did as a boy in Fort Smith. There is some truth in this conclusion.

I am of the firm opinion that we can worship on an old farm in the weedy field of sparrows. We can also honor our origins in the ten-million-dollar cathedral. There is honor in what my sister Ruth terms "bedside Baptist," with televised services for those who wish to be in church, but don't go or can't go and stay home "abed." There are many places and methods of worship in between. I often go to "birdside Baptist" myself.

Herons fill me with wonder, for sure, but I see in them a fine product of the creation, not God the Creator. That is, I don't idolize herons, or in a broader sense, idolize nature. Mostly, birding is my hobby and a profession. At times, birds and birding get me out of myself. I sometimes experience transcendence and otherness. I pass into a different realm without time or object. I gain a sense of the soul.

Folks loyal to more traditional church may also touch or be touched by the spirit. It's a replacement of worldly cares by spirit and wonder. It's the same thing as what I experience, just in a different place and way.

One doesn't grow up in western Arkansas, in a church-going family, without challenges about belief in God, the Bible, and church. Some people seek to put a firm end to this by turning to a different kind of belief—atheism. I've never felt a need for such relief.

God is manifest in rocks, wind, oceans, people, birds. The creative force is revealed most clearly to me in the lives of birds. That's what I mean by God's Second Bible.

On a Sunday afternoon in April several of us with a thirst to see Great Blue Herons have set out west from Springdale. We travel twenty minutes to reach forested hills and the Illinois River, already clothed in the light greens of early spring. We hike along an old farm road, pasture on one side, fern and wildflower-clad limestone bluff on the other. The woods are heavy with grapevines. Greenbriers entangle fallen logs. Masses of white flowered bloodroot cover reddish cherty rubble. Spicebush sports yellow fragrant blooms. The farm road disappears into a marshy overflow bottom.

We are within about two hundred yards of towering sycamores and

Great Blue Heron in July 2010.

cottonwoods. From a shady channel comes ringing *weet weet weet* songs of Prothonotary Warblers, just arrived from a tropical winter in Central and South America. Ahead and above are numerous, large dark masses roughly clustered in the treetops. These are great blues standing in their stick nests.

Hundreds of sticks and twigs are woven into flat-topped masses a yard wide. These are supported in the welcoming, upright limbs that constitute the sycamore's upper crown. Some of last year's sycamore balls hang there, too, decorating budding trees. It's like the dawn of creation, God's Second Bible.

Placed in the tallest trees, these nests are protected from predators and other unwelcomed intrusions. The creek bottom below is rich in small fish, frogs, salamanders, snakes, and crayfish. In such a well-stocked pantry, the parents get enough to eat for themselves and incessantly clamorous heronettes.

We disturb the birds, even at two hundred yards. They have long legs and we fear they could kick eggs or young or both from the nests if the disturbance is too intense. A dozen or more great blues have roughly flushed from atop the stick nests, giving harsh alarm grunts. The birds are unwilling to return as long as we remain. We come up with a count of twenty-seven nests and about the same number of birds.

The remainder of Sunday is devoted to other aspects of God's Second Bible. We find Wood Duck pairs on a shady, hidden pool. A Pileated Woodpecker loudly excavates for beetle larvae within the rotting wood of a downed log. There's an Eastern Phoebe perched in a serviceberry tree above the bluff line. Its *phoebe phoebe* calls carry above the flowing mountain river.

I have a message on my answering machine from Bev and Duane Kepler who live at Beaver in Carroll County. Their place is north of Beaver Lake Dam, but is actually in the headwaters of Table Rock Lake. Both Table Rock and Beaver are impoundments of the much-impounded White River. The Keplers live just above Butler Creek, a Table Rock tributary. Like Osage Creek, Butler has its resident herons. In the middle of March the herons are starting to nest. The reason for the phone call is that Arkansas Department of Highways and Transportation wants to replace an old bridge on Highway 187 paralleling Butler Creek.

Alarm bells have gone off in conservation groups. E-mails are flying. It appears Big Government is hard at work again, potentially crushing wildlife.

It's not that our highway department is officially or even personally insensitive to great blues. They have professional biologists who look into such issues and provide advice to the engineers, who are not, after all, trained in ornithology or ecology.

The problem's context is northwestern Arkansas's growth. People are filtering into rural Carroll County from all over because it's a good place to live and work. Table Rock Lake was impounded in 1958, Beaver in 1966. There were thirteen thousand folks in Carroll County in 1950 and twice that by 2003; growth continues. Ancestral great blues were nesting along Butler Creek before we were riding horses. Now cars are getting larger and heavier. Many people living in rural areas—including my phone callers—commute to work in Eureka Springs, Rogers, even Huntsville. The bridge is unsafe by modern standards. To build a new bridge, part of Highway 187 would be realigned. One choice would move 187 closer to the herons.

The Keplers have questions. Aren't the herons protected? Could the herons survive with the highway so close? Would construction drive them away? What can be done to stop the project?

I head out there with other birders to observe the creek and its birds. Our elegant Great Blue Heron has a penetrating eye. It perches magically atop a stick nest. Behind it I see peeling bark of sycamores and blue timeless sky. We look at bird, bird looks at us. It's a vision maybe from the Pleistocene. It certainly goes back to days when Native American hunters visited Carroll County.

Many busy nests adorn other sycamore trees. It's a heron town above a mountain stream. Like Beaver itself, it's a small community deep in the Ozarks.

The Keplers figure if folks see live birds and nests, they will understand what's at stake. The sight will ignite America's latent decency and respect for wild creatures. People will ride to the rescue of Butler Creek's great blues. I appreciate in a very basic way the spirit and faith of such enterprise. It harkens to revolutionary days, when Colonists rallied against Red Coats.

I imagine highway department folks really dread it. It makes them out to be ogres. It was just a couple of years ago that the highway folks tried to improve the 412 bridge in Madison County over War Eagle Creek, right next door to Carroll County. Bird lovers were astir about a colony of Cliff Swallows whose globular mud nests are attached to the underside of an old bridge. The project stopped until the birds finished nesting.

People love to whack their government and its agencies, and often for good reason. Government after all is a big, unwieldy conglomeration, often insensitive, but by structure, not necessarily by design. By rallying citizens to worthy causes, what people deeply care about may become new government policy, changing the future. We care about Great Blue Herons and choose to protect their nesting sites and habitats. That is, what people feel improves the final product called government, which can act to protect great blues. Anyway, that's the faith enshrined as God's Second Bible.

An adult Great Blue Heron in high breeding plumage at Prairie Creek on Beaver Lake, March 28, 2011, just as nesting season in the Ozarks is under way.

Perhaps we can have a modern bridge and great blues. That's my hope, anyway, though if necessary, I can personally do without the new bridge. This is what I am thinking about as I drive home. I have a funky old, small car about as up to date as the old Beaver bridge. However, I am not commuting to work over it, either.

I recall the heron town over Butler Creek. I remember the modern interstate I drive to work. And the herons, which once had only the White River itself—no small landscape then—now have almost 1300 miles of shoreline along the two lakes. Maybe this will work itself out. And P.S.—cliff swallows nest under the new War Eagle bridge.

It's dogwood season, early May in the Ozarks. Out in the farming country west of Springdale you can hear *pop-pop-pop* of gunfire rolling up through creek bottoms and out across the hayfields. It also rolls up the slopes toward a house. The gunfire sounds faintly like a line of charging infantry in the biannual re-enactment of the Battle of Prairie Grove.

A neighbor calls the law. At first she doesn't understand. She thinks about the Great Blue Herons in the creek bottom. She's been down to the edge of the pasture where they are easily seen. She makes the connection.

Eventually she finds an Arkansas Game and Fish Commission conservation officer. He rolls out in his official law enforcement regalia, but by then the battle is over. It wasn't Prairie Grove, but like the Civil War battle, the dead mark a contemporary battlefield—or I should say, heronry. Wounded birds flop in ferns and wildflowers below sycamores and nests. Incessantly hungry, nestling great blues call from unattended nests high above. Carrying on with business as usual, survivors fly back and forth trying to feed the young.

What Officer Herman finds are spent .22 caliber shell casings. Since the sycamores are rooted in the bottoms below, Herman sees nests only slightly above his line of vision, and fairly close. It looks to him like someone has been sitting in a lawn chair, maybe on a tailgate, and very comfortably firing directly at nests and flying birds. It looks like target practice.

Instead of beer bottles and county road signs as targets, there are Great Blue Herons. There are stationary targets—nestling birds—and flying targets—adult herons. There's no law against target shooting, but there is a law against killing protected birds. What Officer Herman has is a crime scene.

A century ago there was a huge national uproar about shooting herons and egrets. The uproar then was not about using live birds for target practice. Herons and egrets were killed en masse in nesting colonies for their elegant nuptial plumes—special feathers adorning them during courtship and pair formation of the breeding season. The shooters of 1900 invaded nesting colonies in Florida, Louisiana, and elsewhere. Carcasses were plucked for fashionable nuptial plumes. These were sold for the sake of adorning high-fashion women's headgear in the tony markets of Boston and New York.

Folks who take a casual view of killing wild birds might consider what Officer Herman found a few weeks later. It was a Sunday morning. The shooters were back again. So was the neighbor. She wasn't long off the phone before Officer Herman was on the scene arresting a local resident, sixty-seven years old, and two boys, ages fifteen and eighteen, said to be his sons. In Herman's view were thirty dead Great Blue Herons plus numerous shattered eggs. Some nests had been torn apart by rapid-fire shooting. Young birds were squawking on the ground.

Charges against the three came up in Fayetteville Municipal Court. The man and his oldest son were convicted of "theft" and paid $100 fines. Observers counted this as victory for wildlife management since it's rare to catch violators of wildlife laws red-handed. Even if caught, it isn't easy to get convictions against local folks in local courts. Even a run-of-the-mill lawyer knows these are all "good people and they didn't really mean to hurt anything" and "Surely Your Honor won't embarrass this elderly gentleman in front of his children," etc. When I opined that hot-check writers were treated more harshly, Officer Herman stated that two men convicted in a Federal court in Fort Smith for intentionally killing Bald Eagles had received fines less than those levied for littering Arkansas highways.

Officer Herman was quoted in the *Northwest Arkansas Times* as follows: "If I was appalled at the killings, the old man seemed equally appalled that I was actually going to give him a citation for the crime. 'For shooting those old birds?' is how he put it."

I called the old man a couple of months after the legal proceedings. "They're eating up all of our fish," he explained. "Fishing is bad because of these birds." Someone had told him that this was the case. I never found out who told him, but of course there's no doubt that great blues eat many fish. It's also nothing new. Great Blue Herons were eating many fish in the days when "fishing was good," too, and ages and ages before that—before any people were around to claim that they owned all the fish and herons were a threat.

The intentional killing of herons and egrets for the sake of hat adornment was ended in a series of laws culminating with the Migratory Bird Act of 1913. But the intentional killing of herons and egrets has continued, albeit in a new guise.

Commercial catfish and baitfish farming is Big Business in Mississippi, Alabama, Arkansas, Louisiana, and elsewhere. Large-scale rearing operations for catfish and baitfish were few until the late 1960s. Folks that ate catfish—myself and Great Blue Herons included—ate what was caught in creeks and lakes. Back then people ate maybe one-fourth pound of

Cattle Egrets nesting on island in the Arkansas River near Mulberry on July 7, 2011. Commercial slaughter of herons and egrets for elegant feathers associated with the nesting season led to near extinction for several species. Public outcry and protective laws allowed these populations to recover.

catfish per capita. These catfish were truly wild or resulted from lake and stream stocking by state and federal agencies. Good example from northwestern Arkansas: the Craig State Fish Hatchery at Centerton in Benton County started out in 1941 by rearing channel catfish in pure Ozark Mountain water derived from an artesian spring.

By 1995, commercial producers were rearing 440 million pounds of catfish. Today we each eat on average one pound every year. Some folks are still eating wild caught fish, but most of it comes from an estimated 94,000 acres of catfish ponds. These are prime Great Blue Heron feeding opportunities. They are also prime eating opportunities for American White Pelicans, Double-crested Cormorants, Great Egrets and another twenty or so potentially piscivorous (fish-eating) birds. Catfish farmers and fish hatchery operators are up in arms about "freeloading" herons around fish farms and hatcheries.

It's probably of some value here to take complaints by producers about the birds with at least one grain of salt. It's not that the losses aren't real. However, the original home and wintering range for many of these piscivorous birds was within original natural wetlands of the Mississippi River Delta country, 90 percent now converted to croplands and fish farms. All of these birds cannot be shoehorned into the remaining 10 percent. Therefore, it should come as no surprise that commercial fish-rearing operations have, in the eyes and hungers of birds, replaced lost wetlands.

Numbers are all over the board about potential fish losses to birds. The USDA's Animal Damage Control operation estimated in 1997 that individual herons can take an average of twelve fingerling catfish about four inches in length each day. If you figure twenty-two herons spend the year at one fish farm or hatchery, the loss is $3,800 per farm in 1997 dollars. That's big money if you multiply that out for 94,000 acres of fishponds.

These estimates feed a hysteria. It's like Huns in the form of Great Blue Herons and Great Egrets have arrived at the gates of Rome. It's the end of civilization, as we know it.

Whether the rearing ponds are full or drained, they are some of the best places to see birds—for example, twenty or more species of shorebirds that are not piscivorous. Birders value the opportunity to visit these places, but they are also quick to react to killing of birds. When they complain about bird killing, the owners and hatchery operators kick the birders out and figuratively (and sometimes actually) lock the gates.

The crisis atmosphere associated with herons has allowed our federal government via Animal Damage Control to pump up its operations and increase the threat volume: it's Code Red when it comes to herons. Hatchery employees are armed to the teeth for threats posed by herons, cormorants, pelicans, and the rest of the Most Wanted Bad Piscivorous Birds. Universities all over the southeastern United States have graduate students scurrying toward their master's and PhD degrees. They count attempts by herons to catch fish and examine stomach contents. They are studying migration, roosting, and energetics. They erect netting, electrical fences, and all manner of scaring devices that would be met with approval by the Wizard of Oz.

One is forced to conclude that the United States, American fish farmers, and state fish hatchery operators are on the verge of extinction because of the potential ten cents wild birds may add to the cost of an $ 8.95 all-you-can-eat catfish dinner. But even this added cost isn't a certainty.

A dispassionate examination of the situation could allow Code Red to be downgraded to maybe Code Yellow. "Recent research on the similarity in diet and foraging behavior of both herons and egrets raised questions regarding the extent and impact of depredations at catfish farms," wrote authors of a 2003 study. "Most of the catfish taken were in the spring or fall, when catfish diseases were prevalent . . . Studies of captive herons suggested they were inefficient at capturing healthy catfish and subsist mainly on diseased catfish and non-commercial fish (sunfish and shad) in ponds . . . 85% of live catfish captured by Great Blue Herons . . . were diseased and 76% were terminally ill . . . These characteristics of targeting sick fish and congregating at diseased ponds and fingerling ponds limit average losses of healthy fish to less than 1% of total fish stocked" (*Wading Bird Management and Research on North American Aquaculture Facilities,* by B. Dorr and J.D. Taylor II, 2003).

But, of course, facts are not always facts and one does not negotiate with piscivorous terrorists. People in state and federal agencies who want to keep their jobs and climb the career ladder know they can't go easy on Great Blue Herons or other feathered terrorists.

As an alternative to shooting, how about just adding a dime to that $8.95 dinner and stop shooting protected birds? That will go over well at Arkansas Audubon Society, but maybe not with the fish farmers.

Great Blue Herons nest all the way up into Alaska and southern Canada. In winter, they can be found over most of the United States—basically where there is ice-free water. We have them all year in western Arkansas. Data from the annual Christmas Bird Count (CBC) shows them to be present in good numbers within the Fayetteville CBC circle, and even more numerous in the Fort Smith CBC. During the 1990s, for example, the numbers reported for the Fayetteville CBC ranged from ten to twenty-five, whereas at Fort Smith the range was seventeen to seventy-five.

These numbers indicate that habitat is better generally in the Arkansas River Valley at Fort Smith. Temperatures on average are higher in the valley, which means less ice. Most importantly, Fort Smith has natural lakes and streams—the Arkansas River, Poteau River, fine oxbow lake habitat, and many other impoundments.

Great Blue Herons were unreported on the Fayetteville CBC in the 1920s in part because there were no natural lakes, and there was basically no habitat for them within the CBC circle. The 1920s situation is like the current situation on CBCs for the upper Buffalo National River in the 1980s where great blues numbered zero to one most years, with a high count one year of seven. This means that they are along the river, but otherwise there is little habitat.

Today, great blues show up in good numbers on the Fayetteville CBC because since the 1920s every spring and creek, large and small, has been impounded to accommodate human population growth. Every piece of pasture has its pond. None were built to accommodate wintering herons, but herons use them, and we might as well take credit for a positive result.

Some people have even taken things a step further. In this respect, allow me to introduce Larry Nixon, two times BASS Angler of the Year. Writing for *BASS Times* (August 2003), Steve Price reported that Nixon observes the way Great Blue Herons remain motionless for long periods of time, perched on a log or in the shallows, watching and waiting. If a bird flushes, but flies only a short distance, Nixon figures the fishing must be good there. If there are several birds in the area, the signs of good fishing are even better.

According to Price, "The key to understanding the importance of great blues in bass fishing is in realizing these birds rely on larger predator fish to push smaller prey into the shallow water where they may get a chance to nab one. Most of the time those predators are bass."

Nixon shadowed Great Blue Herons for three days of the 1979 Arkansas Bassmaster Invitational at Millwood Lake in southwestern Arkansas. He took forty-four pounds of bass and won.

So who made Great Blue Herons and why? Or for that matter, who made you and me—and why? Why are we all here—the river, the rocks, the trees, the great blues, we who choose to call ourselves birders? I think it comes down to how we see our relationship with God. Since I've been talking so much about God's Second Bible, I feel like I should explain myself a little here.

Pine Siskin harvesting seeds from native sunflowers near Maysville in Benton County on October 31, 2010.

God and I have this special working relationship. I don't ask God who made her, him, or it (your choice), and God doesn't quiz me about the creation. God wants me to consider these things. It's a great burden, our thinking ability. It's one of creation's great marvels. It is supposedly what sets us apart from all other creatures. For that, and much more, I am grateful. Overall, I'm satisfied to note the intricate beauty of Creation, my small personal place in what is obviously a grand design, and let it go at that.

Perhaps that sounds simplistic—"let it go at that," but the word *god* has been so abused and overused its meaning is hard to discern. The word *god* itself is a bumper sticker of sorts, used and misused in so many ways that it has become, for me, a meaningless term or idea. Just consider the bumper sticker slogan, "God Bless America."

It's everywhere: earnest, simple, and patriotic. If we take it at face value on the bumper, we assume the creator of billions of people in hundreds of countries may bless just one country. Blessings stop at our border with Mexico, and wherever the boundary exists off the Atlantic and Pacific coasts. Requested blessings extend to Hawaii, and perhaps to Puerto Rico, even if it is not positioned within the official blessing realm. Are we talking about God here, or just some kind of good-natured patriotism—a hope for the welfare of our country? I'm not at all opposed to the welfare of our country, but why mix God up with that?

The God who created billions of people—most of them who haven't even ever heard of the King James Bible—doesn't turn a backside on everyone except Americans. It troubles me to mix blessings with politics, but I'm not opposed to God blessing all people and countries. That idea doesn't seem political to me.

The question of worship and giving thanks is complicated by what is expected in a culture heavily driven by bumper-sticker logic and religious or faith-based businesses, large and small. There is little space or respect accorded spiritual values outside these prevailing business models. We are suspect if we don't express the correct social views on a bumper sticker or with a spontaneous hallelujah when the stock market goes up or we get a good deal on a used car.

Just as an example, you can go out and wipe out a colony of Great Blue Herons for the fun of shooting, for construction of highways, farms, or housing developments. How many of our churches of the First Bible will condemn these acts against the creation? But these acts will be mourned and often condemned by those who know and understand God's Second Bible.

We have no state-approved religion, but as in certain other countries, our loyalty is suspect unless we present acceptable religious bona fides. We must have approval from the ruling ayatollah, even if that ayatollah is a wealthy television preacher, an American president, the town mayor, or the judge in a public courtroom. In such societies, including our own, if we want our loyalty to remain above reproach, we keep our right hand on the officially approved bible, whether it be the Koran, the Torah, or King James.

Imagine standing up and demanding to take your loyalty oath on a *Peterson Field Guide to the Birds of North America,* claiming that while you understand most folks prefer the King James, you prefer God's Second Bible, and one of its manifestations, a *Sibley Field Guide to Birds.* I say that time has come, and I mean no disrespect for the traditional Holy Bible in saying so.

If we don't buy the approved religious business model, and fail to put "God Bless America" on the bumper, it will be incumbent upon us to prove beyond a reasonable doubt that we are not guilty of something, perhaps atheism. It is not easy to establish such innocence. In some respects, it is easier to be a successful corporate criminal than to be someone who claims spiritual values and beliefs, but declines to warm the official sacred pew of Saturday or Sunday morning. That is, it is more difficult to win acceptance for unorthodox spiritual values than it is to defraud stockholders, using well-aimed political contributions and a right hand firmly on King James.

Great Blue Herons show up at their nesting colonies in early spring. The first activity in the heronry involves birds staking out their claims by standing up in old nests from previous years. Some observers have stated that the males and females may gather for dancing in a pasture nearby. I have never seen this myself, but I have seen them slowly flapping their great wings up and down as they circle round and round, something like dancing school children.

John James Audubon once observed what he termed a dance. "The males walk about with an air of great dignity," he noted, "bidding defiance to their rivals, and the females croak to invite the males to pay their addresses to them."

After the pairing comes nest refurbishment. This mainly consists of adding fresh sticks to the bulky platforms of last year. If the birds are left in peace, there will be another generation of great blues. The long string of time, stretching back into the sun and beginnings, moves into futures. This is the plan, as I understand it, according to God's Second Bible.

Amy Edie in Mount Sequoyah Woods Park, Fayetteville, on January 16, 2011.

On an occasional Sunday my friend Amy Edie invites me to go with her to an assisted-living retirement facility in Fayetteville. She loves to sing the old Protestant hymns adored by retirees, ages seventies to nineties. On these Sundays she gathers up her handmade booklets that include lyrics of popular hymns. She printed the pages in big easily readable type. She also takes a rich-sounding old acoustic guitar and her friendly little dog Hattie who is fond of being petted and is therefore popular among the retirees.

Amy greets and smiles, and radiates the magnetic energy of a woman in her early forties. She bounds down the halls to individual rooms, personally inviting Mildred, Dolores, Bob, Madge, Virginia, Julia, and more than a dozen others, plus anyone just sitting around the lobby. They come on canes, in wheelchairs, or walking with one another, with the best walker supporting the other.

It's not hard to round up a circle of singers because many folks sang in the choirs or played piano in the churches of their youth. I get the impression that Amy's show is less about church and more about tradition. These elders remember fifty years ago or more, when they were raising children, teaching school, when they were themselves sons and daughters. Amy's songs link them to these now distant treasures.

Probably the best singer in the whole bunch, Dolores, suffers from severe short-term memory loss, but she hasn't forgotten music and she sings with gusto. She sang in the church choir and played piano and organ. I have heard her play the piano and she still plays well. She knows all the hymns by heart. The numbers and letters in Amy songbooks don't register with her, but she knows melodies and words inscribed on her heart fifty years ago.

My invitation to sing with Amy grew out of a canoe trip on the Buffalo River when we found that we knew many of the same songs. For a while, we paddled the Buffalo to the beat of "The Old Rugged Cross" and a few songs by Bob Dylan, another Amy favorite. It's like I'm a kid at Grand Avenue Baptist in Fort Smith. Well, not just like—I have a paddle in hand, not a songbook. I'm wearing a bathing suit, old shirt, and a floppy sun hat RATHER than suit and tie and shiny black pointy toed uncomfortable Sunday-go-to-meeting shoes.

OK, so maybe it's not so easy to visualize how anyone paddling the Buffalo River could sing about the Crucifixion. But there it was, on a lovely June day, on water so clear you could see fingerling bass against multicolored pebbles.

I have heard it alleged that God works in mysterious ways. The first Bible—the Holy Bible—is, I suppose, set in stone. You can never be so sure about the Second Bible. It has a way of expressing itself in unorthodox but thrilling and modestly reverent ways. Maybe it's the flight of a Great Blue Heron, or sung praises in a retirement community, or maybe just the simplicity of a Sunday paddle stroke on the Buffalo.

This is a view of the campus of the University of Arkansas in Fayetteville during heavy snow in February 2011. The picture is taken from Wilson Park, and Old Main seems to rise above the storm.

The Golden Calf

When the people saw that Moses delayed to come down from the mountain, the people assembled about Aaron and said, "Come, make us a god who will go before us; as for this Moses, the man who brought us up from the land of Egypt, we do not know what has become of him." Aaron said to them, "Tear off the gold rings which are in the ears of your wives, your sons, and your daughters, and bring them to me." He fashioned them into a molten calf and they said, "This is your god . . ."

—Exodus 32

THERE'S A GOLD rush underway in western Arkansas. It's a little like California in 1848 and the Yukon in 1897. Business is booming. The numbers on those green population signs at the city limits are constantly moving up.

Our gold is called "quality of life." We are in the "Sun Belt," a blessed place since the invention of air-conditioning. We are celebrated in glossy magazines as one of the Ten Best Places to Live in America. We have low crime and low taxes, which makes us retirement dynamite.

We've never had anything but apples and chickens here, so we don't have many Love Canal pollution bombs, or at least any that we know about right now. Boy, we have lots of shopping, a huge football arena, and lots of minimum-wage jobs. Like my father used to say, we're packing 'em in like mackerels.

The white gleaming eminence that is the Northwest Arkansas Mall was once a mere twinkle in the developer's eyes. That was in the 1960s when the mall was a hilltop cow pasture on the edge of Johnson, overlooking north Fayetteville and south Springdale. It was much like that mythical day in 1849, just before John Sutter discovered California gold. We were not where major highways join. We had no Walmarts, no chain theme restaurants, no auto parks, no massed phalanxes of financial institutions, no specialty hospitals, no smorgasbord of doctor's offices. We were not the center of the economic universe.

As a pre-Mall U of A student of the early 1960s, I walked from the University of Arkansas campus to aging red brick buildings on Fayetteville's old-fashioned square. There I shopped for clothing, books, and watched movies. Highway 71 skirted downtown Fayetteville. Now roll things forward ten years. I have a college degree. The big hill between Fayetteville and Springdale has been dozed down. Red clay dirt and gray limestone rocks are trucked off to fill nearby natural wetlands, making them suitable for real estate empires.

Abracadabra: old Highway 71 becomes "71 B" and 71 proper is now a freeway looping around the west side of Fayetteville, just below—but well within earshot—of the university campus. Northwest Arkansas Mall has risen white brick by white brick on the flattened hill.

Smart people with smart money know what's ahead. Abracadabra: the freeway conveniently rejoins 71 B where the mall is being constructed. Meanwhile, many of the old-style red-brick buildings on the old Fayetteville Square are razed. Razing the square is termed "urban renewal." Building the mall is "progress." Like California in 1849, like the Yukon in 1897, the gold rush is on. Just like in Bible days, we can't wait to have the gold of our natural history melted down and fashioned into the new golden calf.

There's lots more gold to be stripped off the Ozarks for this new golden calf. Like the miners of '49 and '97, our commercial leaders immediately begin stripping a familiar kind of gold from our streams. Developers put bulldozers hard at work flattening the bottomland fields along Mud Creek where Fayetteville and Springdale join. They uproot all of the riparian forest—the white oaks, shagbark hickories, sycamores, buttonbush, and willows. Then they put the dozers at work directly within the creek, straightening and deepening the channel. This accomplished, they cover the reshaped creek banks and what's left of the channel with huge chunks of limestone, blasted from hilltop pits.

Thus is born the heart and soul of the new western Arkansas empire, capital of the Best Place to Live in America. We have flat, dry, commercially rich ground in place of a stream with a tendency to flood out into fields and form wetlands. Real-estate offices and banks rise upon the floodplain forest in place of willows and Wood Ducks.

When people protest, our captains of development respond that Mud Creek under their management is more beautiful than it had ever been in nature. Flush with their new golden calf, our civic leaders bow down and pronounce it all good.

The White River hills give rise to perennial streams flowing west, eventually joining the Illinois River ten miles east of Fayetteville. Lake Fayetteville, for example, is an impoundment of Clear Creek, rising near Sonora east of Springdale. Mud Creek rises east of Fayetteville and flows just south of the modern Northwest Arkansas Mall. Clabber Creek originates in a natural spring flow protected by a culvert under modern I-540 near the University's Agricultural Experimental Farm.

The former mall hill stands above Mud Creek in the south, Clear Creek to the north, Clabber Creek to the west. It rises above—not Fayetteville-Springdale-Rogers-Bentonville—but a veritable Northwest Arkansas City. Its symbol: the golden calf of progress.

Flowing springs and rainwater feed the streams. By the time they reach the Highway 71 B corridor, they are flowing through grassy valleys and some of the lowest-lying land in northwestern Arkansas. Common in these valleys are seasonal wetlands whose clay-rich prairie soils hold rainwater and support marshy vegetation like sedges and associated birds like bitterns and rails. They were rarely plowed in the past because of all the water, which also impeded other kinds of development. They were fairly good as pasture and were mainly used for this purpose—until the gold rush.

In historic times, extremely dry weather included wild fires that spread across the old prairies. This favored prairie grasses like big bluestem and Indian grass. Fires also fostered development of open groves dominated by post oaks, blackjack oaks, and hickories. These forests occurred on ground slightly higher than the surrounding stream

Present in western Arkansas throughout the year, American Goldfinch is the symbol for Northwest Arkansas Audubon Society. Here one is foraging on ripe seeds from native sawtooth sunflowers near Maysville in Benton County on October 31, 2010.

bottomlands. Old timers called them oak barrens or prairie woods. Typically, barrens were open and park-like and also contained prairie grasses.

The fields and associated shrubs had nesting populations of Northern Bobwhites, Greater Prairie-Chickens, Bell's Vireos, Yellow-breasted Chats, Eastern Meadowlarks, Painted Buntings, and Dickcissels. The barrens hosted Red-tailed Hawks, Northern Bobwhites, Mourning Doves, Red-headed Woodpeckers, Eastern Wood-Pewees, Eastern Bluebirds, Blue-gray Gnatcatchers, Summer Tanagers, and others. Bison grazed the fields and the barrens.

As they loop around north Fayetteville, I-540 travelers pass over and near seasonally wet former prairies and associated oak barrens. They pass over the perennial flow of Wilson Springs and its population of Arkansas Darters, a small rare fish. This area is smack in the middle of the gold rush.

The gold rush has brought with it many improvements in our way of life, including a novel urban forest. Oaks, hickories, sycamores, and willows are replaced with Bradford pear trees, rising star in urban environments. Bradford's many benefits include being compact and uniform in shape, disease resistant, easily cared for, and perhaps more to the point, a bit of green midst universal asphalt. You can buy it just about anywhere, and even those who lack a green thumb will be hard pressed to kill one. In short, it is a dozer-proof tree, developer's dream, greenish curtain covering radical changes. It's apparently a tree better adapted to current events than native oaks, hickories, and sycamores. It's called progress for those excited by new restaurants, clubs, shops, and cheerful boxes like Walmart and Target.

Many folks don't notice the old post oaks going down and huge parking lots going up, because they are watching a big Tyson's truck pass them, mentally preparing for shopping, reliving last night's fight with the spouse, or fumbling with the CD player, one eye on the road and one eye on the dashboard. That's what generally happens to me, anyway.

In the spring of 2000, plans were moving ahead for commercial development of a highly visible and strategically located oak barren in the Mud Creek area south of the Northwest Arkansas Mall. Initially, it appeared that all of the eighty-one century-old trees would be preserved. As development proceeded, it was clear that over half would be lost. Members of the public—"environmentalists" is the general descriptive term—and the developer's representatives jockeyed over tree-protection rules. City council meetings became contentious. Some citizens remembered Mud Creek's flattening and straightening in the 1970s.

To Mary Lightheart, a resident of Goshen, it seemed Fayetteville's tree-protection ordinance was meaningless if the grove could be cut. On May 4, 2000, Lightheart climbed one of the larger trees and vowed to remain there. She stayed two weeks, with a large ground-support crew, and a fair amount of public support, judging from packed city council meetings and petitions signed by 1,600 supporters.

Her protest struck a nerve, both pro and con. It became front-page news in the local papers. Judging from the developer's representatives, you would have thought her tree sitting was the end of the world as we know it. To supporters, she was Saint Mary of the Blessed Oaks.

Lightheart's tactic of sitting in someone else's tree to try and save the best of the Ozarks might seem radical, but reverence for old trees in our growing town is as patriotic as Mom and apple pie. It's almost a citizenship requirement, like baseball and hotdogs. That is, Mary Lightheart and her tree sitting is only a new wrinkle in an ancient tradition. Upsets about the cutting of trees in the pathway of "progress" is a Fayetteville tradition dating back more than a century. Considering that, it's amazing there was no tree preservation ordinance until 1993.

A former mayor shed tears, figuratively at least, when a black oak was cut to make way for sidewalks and widening on Dickson Street in 1888. Mayor J. H. Van Hoose wrote it all up for the *Washington County Review* in August 1888.

The wonders of modern transportation had come to Fayetteville in the nature of a railroad in 1881, much like I-540 a century later. The *Review* records that city fathers determined the downtown square needed connecting to the Arkansas Industrial University (now the U of A) with sidewalks and a widened Dickson Street. Much as the grove south of Northwest Arkansas Mall is today in the path of commercial development, in 1888 the black oak familiar to the pioneers of 1828 stood in the way on Dickson Street.

"Some of the citizens on this street regretted very much to give up their nice shade trees, and we cannot blame them, for a spreading green tree is a good friend these hot days," Mayor Van Hoose wrote on that long ago August day. In the days before air conditioning and inside-the-Mall shopping, those two little words "August" and "day" had significance. "But the tree that cost the most money and sweat to say nothing of tears, was a gigantic old, black oak which stood in Mr. Prentice's front yard at the junction of Block and Dickson Streets.

"This tree was one of the original landmarks on Prairie Hill, which was the Indian name for this locality before old Capt. Magarah built his first log cabin here. Sixty years ago this hill and these surroundings were not covered with timber as we now have always been accustomed to see them, but at wide intervals there could be seen only a solitary tree dotting the prairie. This old oak of which I speak was one of the first that took root on the prairie."

Prairie Hill (roughly the town square and environs) was Prairie Township's center, the entirety of Fayetteville in 1828. There had been bison here in 1819 and Native American hunters following them. Undoubtedly, it was also a Greater Prairie-Chicken dancing ground. There were no golden calves here then.

In 1828, trees were confined to spring runs, such as that at the corner of today's Spring and Willow Streets, where the first cabin was built. There were only scattered groves of hardy oaks, such as that on Dickson Street in Van Hoose's time. The grove south of the mall—where in May 2000 an energetic grandmother named Mary Lightheart caused so much anxiety with her tree sitting—was basically a foreign country, with visits from hunters and Passenger Pigeons.

Few modern residents realize how much the landscape has changed. One never hears about Prairie Hill and not one in a thousand of the residents in 2011 can explain why it's named Prairie Township. ("Huh? Prairie? I don't see no stinkin' prairie.") Most can probably give directions to Northwest Arkansas Mall.

There was quite a fuss too, in 1954, when in order to make way for progress on College Avenue, a huge tulip tree was taken down at the corner of Lafayette and College. The *NWA Times* thought that this tree might have been the oldest tree planted in Fayetteville. "Some public concern over its demise has been expressed."

If you have lived in Fayetteville for a long time and know any of the older residents, you learn that College Avenue was once-upon-a-time shady and tree-lined. Within their memories much of this street, named for a pre–Civil War pioneering educational institution, Arkansas College, has become a noisy eyesore, chief thoroughfare of Northwest Arkansas City. Few residents of our gold rush–era Northwest Arkansas City can tell you anything about that pre–Civil War college that gave the town much of its original character. For that information you must contact volunteers who staff the nearby Tebbetts house, headquarters of the Washington County Historical Society, a long ways from Northwest Arkansas Mall.

From all of this you can see that "some public concern over its demise" is a Fayetteville tradition, patriotic as "calling the hogs" in

Razorback Stadium. There was "concern expressed" when in the 1980s giant pines were cut on campus to make way for the Engineering Center and when in the 1990s trees and a hoped-for Dickson Street park were flattened for the Walton Arts Center parking lot. There was outrage when mature oaks were cut at the corner of Garland and North. Folks had long thought this would remain green space, a buffer for development around Oak Plaza and nearby Leverett Elementary School.

Mayor Van Hoose helped fell the old oak in 1888. Current mayors, figuratively speaking, helped fell the oak grove south of the mall by casting their lot with the developers. It's all progress for those who consider Bradford pears as reasonable trade for black oaks and post oaks.

Pioneer oaks were falling in 1888 to make way for a modern street between the town and the campus and a railroad that linked Fayetteville to the world. Most of a grove of pioneer oaks came down in 2000 to make way for national retailers who will sell their goods in Northwest Arkansas City, the unincorporated entity Mayor Van Hoose could not have imagined.

I haven't seen any golden calves for sale in these stores. But you know the time can't be too far off. As they say, the market is there.

As far as I know, there is no inherent sin in Bradford pears, or other ornamental trees that are planted in place of our oaks. But I doubt protests would erupt if it was a grove of Bradford pears flattened on behalf of a Kohl's, Target, or Walmart Supercenter. People protest the destruction of native trees because they are links in our shared history. Creatures of mass consumerism and the asphalt country, Bradford pears and cousin ornamentals breath carbon monoxide, are decorated by wind-blown Walmart bags and serve as unappreciated stand-ins for natural beauty. They have their value and they have my sympathy, but they contain nothing of the old prairie. Unlike mature oaks, they will never support nests of that scion of Prairie Hill, the Red-tailed Hawk. They do not link us to the time of the bison, the prairie-chicken, or the Native Americans.

According to Henry Thoreau, "If a man walks in the woods for the love of them . . . for half his days, he is esteemed a loafer; but if he spends his whole day as a speculator, shearing off those woods, he is esteemed industrious and enterprising—making the earth bald before its time."

Of course Thoreau was notoriously no fan of progress in the

These hoot owls, actually Barred Owls, commonly reside in forests throughout western Arkansas, including those in urban areas. This bird was roosting on a short limb projected from a large tree on April 19, 2009.

Boston area in the 1850s. He lived in a nondescript cabin frequented by Wood Thrushes, alongside a pond known mainly by Common Loons and water snakes. He didn't have any golden calves in his cabin, or heart.

Arkansas darters, a lovely, two-inch long native fish, look like gold in the shallow clear water where they live. They are found in the state in

Crawfish can be sensitive indicators of water quality. Master Naturalist Joan Reynolds checking for crawfish in shallow pools on Steel Creek, near confluence with the Buffalo River, on July 21, 2011.

just a few springs. Their rarity has earned them a privileged place on lists of protected species maintained by the Arkansas Natural Heritage Commission. Darters made the local news after they were found in Fayetteville by biologist Steve Wilson in the early 1970s. He was working for the Arkansas Department of Highways and Transportation during construction of I-540. Two spring flows emerged from a slope just below the University of Arkansas farm, then flowed westerly toward junction with Clabber Creek. The springs were right in the highway's path. A tunnel (or casement) was built to protect springs and fish. Informally, the place was named Wilson Springs. There matters stood for almost two decades.

I visited Wilson Springs in early May of 1982. Near the spring run I heard the distinctive song of Bell's Vireo: *cheedle cheedle cheedle chee? cheedle cheedle cheedle chew!* Hidden in dense bushes along the spring run, the singer was no doubt unaware that Fayetteville—once confined to Prairie Township—was now becoming Northwest Arkansas City. The singer who had sung for the old prairie grasslands sang now for commuters and eighteen-wheelers.

Low conical hummocks, or prairie mounds, distinguished the shrubby fields. On these mounds were masses of brilliant orange-reddish flowers called Indian paintbrush. Like the first songs of Bell's Vireo newly arrived in Fayetteville from their winter quarters in the south, paintbrush is a sign of spring, of prairie renewal, emblem of Fayetteville's history.

In the field beyond the spring I found an Eastern Meadowlark nest with four eggs, a Red-tailed Hawk nest with a well-grown chick, two more Bell's Vireos, a Yellow-breasted Chat, and other grassland and shrubland birds like migrating Savannah Sparrows and White-crowned Sparrows. The spring and surrounding fields was a green space, but thin and rapidly diminishing, along what was becoming I-540.

The spring runs a few hundred yards below an old prairie grove, then junctions with Clabber Creek. Unfortunately, like Mud Creek to the east, Clabber had been heavily prospected for developer's gold. Oaks, hickories, redbuds, and sycamores had been dozed out of the way. Clabber Creek was deepened and straightened. Even this treatment didn't suit the developers, who still saw too much water and all the development costs associated with getting that water out of the way.

Abracadabra: developers unloaded 289 acres with springs, rare fish and wet fields on the City of Fayetteville in 1990. The theory at the time went something like this: under benign civic influence—and with only the good of the people in mind—the transaction was touted as a public goldmine. Fayetteville had a 1950s style industrial park in the south part of town. This would become the north industrial park, adjacent the university, a potential "high technology" industrial park. The underlying financial principle was that it would be easier for the city to use taxpayer funds to fill and otherwise develop wetlands than for private interests to use their own funds.

In 1994, students from the University of Arkansas's American Fisheries Society chapter became voluntary stewards of the darter and seven acres. Andrea Radwell, a graduate fisheries student in biological sciences, became the group's mainspring. By 2002 she had become convinced that protecting just seven acres could not save Arkansas darters. She noted that development plans included destruction of adjoining

Fish Crows, one of two crow species in western Arkansas, are most often associated with river bottoms and other bodies of water. Their calls have a nasal quality, as though they have a southern accent or a stopped up nose. This photograph is from July 2010.

wetlands, recharge areas for the springs. No adjoining wetlands equals no healthy flowing spring. She pointed out that the city government had spent generously on engineering studies aimed at development, but spent nothing aimed at protecting the springs. It's simple math and science grasped easily by undergraduate biology majors. Not so easily grasped by those who worship the golden calf.

Andrea at first worked closely with the city government on spring protection. But as things heated up, she networked with all who would listen. She encouraged local environmental groups to look into the situation. The gold rush was on at Wilson Springs, just as in the time when Mary Lightheart sat in her mother tree.

I became friends with a Chicago native and skilled student of birds, Mike Mlodinow, back in the early 1980s, about the time I first saw Wilson Springs. That's Mike with a mass of dark curly hair and beard, and binoculars hung around his neck. He's the guy you've seen for two decades walking around Fayetteville, especially forested places like Markham Hill and Mount Sequoyah. He's the guy who goes out to Gregory Park, but not for an ice cream cone at McDonald's. He's walking around in Evergreen Cemetery, but not necessarily to visit the graves of Fayetteville's pioneer families, or those of the famous, like Senator J. William Fulbright. He takes the bus out to bird University Farm. There he inspects the crops, but he's looking for Smith's Longspur, not soybeans.

It looks kind of like Mike is bird watching, and I guess in one sense that's what he's doing. But actually, he's a gold miner like all the rest of us. He's out day after day collecting bird data. He collects numbers to crunch when he gets home. He's trying to discover, in a very specific way, which bird species prefer which places, and at what time of the year they exhibit such preferences. He's looking for patterns. That's the gold in his birding.

Bird study has long been his gold standard. He had his first formal encounter with birds during second grade when he was assigned a poster and chose for it—well, you know what. He was going out on formal birding trips by the seventh grade. He and his brothers shared a pair of binoculars. He got his first personal binoculars in high school. Birds carried him to a master's degree. He then moved to Fayetteville for further studies at the University of Arkansas.

For years he drove a 1976 Mercury Cougar maintained in running order by the grace and skills of a shade-tree mechanic who lived next door. But even with that benefit, the Cougar died around Christmas in 1995. Mike cares a great deal more about birds than cars, and when the Cougar was junked, he began to walk and take public transit to his favorite birding places. Increasingly, his birding was focused on the best spots nearest town. That eventually brought him to Wilson Springs.

Mike is a leader in the local group of birders who conduct the annual Fayetteville Christmas Bird Count. We now have fifty-odd years of carefully collected field data on winter birds in the Fayetteville area. The count itself serves as an information center, a place where those with an interest in birds find others with similar interests. In 2000 there was talk about the low wet fields along Dean Solomon Road—the west side of the Wilson Springs property. These winter fields yielded Sedge

Wrens and Marsh Wrens, plus Le Conte's and Lincoln's Sparrows—all birds difficult to find at midwinter and on the Fayetteville CBC.

Mike birded Wilson Springs during the spring and summer of 2001. He found Dickcissels, Bell's Vireos, Painted Buntings, and most significantly, Henslow's Sparrow, a very rare nesting bird anywhere in Arkansas. He found them out in those big fields giving their simple, two-noted song. It goes like this: *chi-lick! chi-lick!* It was a significant discovery. Mike looked for birders who would help him collect more data.

As Mike continued his bird studies during 2001 and 2002, it became evident that the 289 acres of city property supported a surprisingly diverse group of prairie flora and grassland birds, including Henslow's Sparrow. It supported them even though the east side of the property bordering I-540—where I found Indian paintbrush and Bell's Vireo in 1982—had been destroyed, ecologically speaking. It supported them despite the channeling and straightening of Clabber Creek.

Nationally, 32 million acres of native grasslands have been converted to non-native fescue pastures, towns, farms, and roads. Indian paintbrush has been plowed and bulldozed, and prairie mounds flattened. In the process, birds that evolved in native grasslands have been in steep decline.

Not everyone shared this concern. A memo circulating around the city administration written by an engineer undermined the aquatic concerns raised by Andrea Radwell and cast doubt on the reality of issues brought forward by bird watchers and other citizens. The mayor was encouraged to push ahead with the tech-park plan. He was also advised to give special names to the streets built over wetlands. One street, for example, could be named Henslow Sparrow Drive, another, Arkansas Darter Drive.

In reading this memo, it's unclear if this advice to the mayor was tongue-in-cheek, or if the engineer had been so blinded by the golden calf that he believed this was a helpful idea. Or if it was just pure blind cynicism.

Building and developing is a perfectly respectable and often useful occupation. However, for many years it has been something of a civic religion, heavily proselytized by Fayetteville's leaders both in and out of government. It has become our Official Religion and the golden calf our Official Idol. It leads to cynical thinking like that expressed in the memo. This is such a deep-rooted faith that those who express different beliefs—Mary Lightheart and Andrea Radwell come to mind here—are viewed as unreasonable.

I joined Mike in his bird studies. By May 10, 2002, we had documented 123 bird species within the 289 acres. Among them were 18 considered of "Special Concern" on lists maintained by Partners-In-Flight, a national coalition working for bird conservation. In other words, Wilson Springs retained both the real gold of native fish and native birds despite a lot of plowing, dozing, and all sorts of rough handling.

The issue came to head when then-mayor Dan Coody appointed a special task force to sort through the complex economic and biological issues. He picked the task force from among those who had helped him win office: Sierra Club, University professors, real-estate developers, and engineers. The task force was to advise him on a proper course of action. They heard from the Mud Creek miners and those who had channelized Clabber Creek, business owners, and private citizens. Over the course of several public hearings, everyone who had anything to add to the discussion was given the microphone. It was participatory democracy, a kind of civic gold in action. We assumed the mayor would honor its recommendations.

In the fall of 2002, the task force recommended that up to approximately 219 acres of the property be preserved to protect springs, Arkansas darters, and the birds. The task force wanted the Clabber Creek bottomlands to continue to serve as a rainwater sponge—for the recharge of the springs and for protection of downstream properties from flooding.

About seventy acres of obvious dry uplands that front I-540 on an existing service road were considered suitable for commercial development. The value of those seventy acres was estimated to be enough to offset costs incurred by the city since the 1990 purchase.

Mike and I continued to go birding there. The list edged up to 130 species. We were starting to think about trails and birding tours.

Andrea Radwell was thinking about long-term darter management. She also looked at studies of the endemic Osage burrowing crawfish, common in the wet fields. I wondered if we could restore Tallgrass Prairie habitat in some areas that retained patches of Indian

Once common in prairie habitats, ornate box turtles have now become quite rare as a result of habitat loss in northwestern Arkansas. This one was at Stump Prairie near Siloam Springs on April 28, 2009.

grass, big bluestem, and switch grass. Joe Woolbright, founder of Ozark Ecological Restoration—who is restoring prairies elsewhere in northwest Arkansas—came out to help.

Compromise solutions to contentious issues can encourage new thinking and even dreams. Cynicism can destroy faith in government.

Former mayor Dan Coody is part of the "green" generation, and he has both courage and vision. I was at a meeting once where he pulled out his Visa card to show us that his charges benefited the Sierra Club. It seemed funny to me at the time, but I understood his point. He has put muscle of his office behind additions to the city's parks. These efforts are certainly one of his legacies. He publicly dreamed and worked in behalf of bikeways that would allow residents easy and healthful access to the entire city. Under his mayoralty, these bikeways began to take formal shape with a lot of opposition from those who said we couldn't afford them.

Coody and his spouse attended Andrea Radwell's wedding and were considered good friends. Well-heeled friends of mine held fundraising house parties when he ran for office. Mike Mlodinow frequently birds on the southeast side of Mount Sequoyah, where Coody built a subdivision of attractive, tree-shaded homes before becoming mayor. The area is affectionately called Coodyville. During his birding walks, Mike got to know the mayor, his spouse, and the mayor's mother.

Northwest Arkansas's environmentalist community gave him their votes and provided the edge that allowed him to defeat the incumbent. They were impressed by Coody's sensitivity to environmental issues. They wanted a city administration that was independent of developer's interests. That is, they didn't want more mayors blinded by the reflections from a golden calf.

But the gold rush gets in and under the skin of all of us. It's like we breathe it. There is this almost religious belief whose faith evaluates land in its dollar value per square foot. What is in their view wasteland, supporting only hawks and meadowlarks, would be transformed, Rumpelstiltskin-like, into a potential goldmine.

Caught between these viewpoints and recommendations of his task force, the mayor bailed. He used his governmental authority to sell the 289 acres to a developer in Rogers. He said the money raised in the sale would make it possible to buy parkland of higher quality elsewhere. It would help fund bikeways.

In the end, about 120 acres of the original 289 were placed in a conservation trust, a sort of public-private partnership. A potential urban park of this magnitude is nothing to sneeze at. There could be trails and Arkansas darters in the preserved area. No doubt, Mike and I and a hopefully growing Northwest Arkansas Audubon Society would go birding there.

Fayetteville has thrown away several of its breeding bird species, including a rare one, Bachman's Sparrow. It will now be next to impossible to hear the soothing whistles of Northern Bobwhites. There will be

Ebony jewelwing, a species of damselfly, where waterfalls flow into Piney Creek at Ninestone Land Trust in Carroll County, July 8, 2011.

fewer of the magnificent Painting Buntings. People who worked hard to protect Arkansas darters have less confidence about its future.

There are also small victories to claim. It won't help the future to forget them now.

These fights galvanize a small but important community that values preservation of wild habitat over golden calves. They favor protecting biological processes. They are willing to invest themselves in cajoling fellow town folk into thinking whole earth thoughts. Let's include the big picture in our thinking. We can have a healthy economy and a healthy environment.

If we can't keep "big box" development out of the old prairie grove, we can create psychological space within our government to enforce the existing environmental rules. We can encourage some folks within the golden calf-worshipping–pro-development groups to support more protection for natural habitats.

To put this in plain English, a business planning to pave over seasonal wetlands at Wilson Springs is going to learn that many folks value Osage burrowing crawfish more than another big-box store. Many would prefer that wetlands not be turned into parking lots. Maybe some of those who worship the golden calf will discover that it is not good business to be an environmental deadbeat.

Sure, hardcore true believers at the foot of the golden calf will never yield an inch. I can hear them singing now: "Level every mountain / Straighten every stream / Pave every wetland / Until you own the entire thing." I'm just kidding, of course. But others not so fixed in their beliefs will take a second look. They will begin to listen. They will slowly learn that Arkansas darters are their heritage. Someday they—or one of their kids—may know that an interesting and beautiful creature, Henslow's Sparrow, once nested within the city limits of Fayetteville. That newly found sensitivity may find a good home—if not here, then elsewhere.

Mary Lightheart's perch in what she called Mother Tree is history. What you see today from I-540 are football-field size asphalt parking lots—that's where the Greater Prairie-Chickens were in pioneer times. The big box stores—Kohl's and Target—were constructed, but room was left for part of the prairie grove. If you really work your imagination, you can see Passenger Pigeons as they sweep over the old prairie toward the desirable small post oak acorns. The grove's remnant is there, traditional Ozark trees with their very own numbered tags. We may still claim the dream space, even if we don't have title to the land.

As far as I know, in the year of our lord 2011, Arkansas darters swim in Wilson Springs. Somewhere in that 120 acres of possible preservation is room for Indian grass and burrowing crawfish. National Audubon and its state organization, Audubon Arkansas, are partners in a plan to manage the remaining 120 acres, acres where the golden calf will hopefully find no home. Painted Buntings may show again. Clabber Creek and Mud Creek are not what they were before the gold rush, but they remain opportunities.

Ducks during a freeze-up at Craig State Fish Hatchery in Centerton in January 2011. Buffleheads swim in icy water, Gadwalls and a male Northern Shoveler stand on the ice.

November

"A lake is the landscape's most beautiful and expressive feature. It is the earth's eye; looking into which the beholder measures the depth of his own nature . . ."

—Thoreau

SOUTHWARD BLASTS OF Arctic manufacture race past Nome, Alaska, and Fargo, North Dakota, headed south. Six inches of snow blankets the Black Hills of South Dakota. The flint hills of Kansas are in flurries and polar air rushes into western Arkansas. It could be the second week in November or a little later. Harsh weather equals good birds.

Under fresh cold winds, leaves that painted western Arkansas a riot of color in October pulsate and drop. It's goodbye fall, hello winter. Sweetgum and maple leaves drop free, riding the blast.

I am sailing, too, to find my winter stuff: long johns and stocking caps, heavy gloves, and insulated boots. I'm checking my gas furnace to make sure it still works. I've got my binoculars and spotting scope ready to go. I'm making a thermos of hot coffee for what is bound to be a long cold day.

Gone now is the Great North Country's green prairie summer. Treeless Arctic tundra wears ice and snow attire. Hidden lakes where loons nest freeze shut. Ice slips across cattail-lined prairie pothole ponds and marshy sloughs. It's the great avian shake-out and good birding is heading our way.

November's heavens have suddenly opened.

Bald Eagles are heading south from their Alaskan nesting stronghold.

Ditto for hardy Ring-billed Gulls, soaring ahead of the polar onslaught. Tens of thousands of six-inch-long Lapland Longspurs empty grassy fields of their flight rattles and musical *tee-lee-oos*. They settle in northwestern Arkansas. There will be big flocks of American Pipits, too, bobbing and tail-wagging in crop fields, their sharp *pipit-pipit* calls overhead.

Snow Buntings, a real rarity in Arkansas, have been reported just to the north, in Missouri. Will this be a Snowy Owl flight year? What is our chance of finding Rough-legged Hawks? Windows that rattle menacingly under cold blasts promise bonanza birding.

Ducks old and young head south. Old drakes and hens may be in the range of three to six years, but occasional birds are older than ten. Claiming for avian royalty a new land, young-of-the-year make their first trip south. Masses of polar air add speed and power their rapid flight from bitter cold and ice. South-south they slip, south through cold, inky black. And lo, with the opening of a wintry day, our western Arkansas ponds and lakes are transformed: drake Mallards all festive green and ruddy chests; Northern Pintails with upraised tail feathers; Gadwall flocks flashing bold white wing patches; white heads and chests of Buffleheads rising and falling among gray, wind-whipped waves.

In the distance, and in deep water, swim long-billed, low-slung Common Loons. Pied-billed Grebes dive and disappear. Here and there are white heads of Horned Grebes and even a few Eared Grebes. Sometimes, on the nastiest of days—when no coat and no pair of gloves suffice, when teeth hurt from the cold, when if we were practical or smart we wouldn't be here at all—on such days we may get lucky and spot the big sea duck, Surf Scoter, or maybe the black head, long white neck and big yellow beak of a Western Grebe.

White head against the dark wooded shoreline, a Bald Eagle watches the action from its perch on a snag, above. Below, American Coots actively forage, bills white like the eagle's head.

Come November, it's time to take in hand the spotting scope, binoculars, field guide, and head to the lake of choice. It's time to set the old eyeball firmly and resolutely onto the scope's eyepiece, even if the wind is sharp, even if you have to perch under an umbrella. Waterfowl fly south when snow flies up north. The lake may be fogged-over, but as a morning breeze begins to disperse the fog, it's plain that tundra and prairie potholes are poorer, western Arkansas richer. Canada is blanketed with snow, western Arkansas is blanketed with migrants.

It's November. Snow Geese have been flying all night. It's time to zip up the coat and head for the lake.

A traveler here a century ago, or even a thousand years ago, would have seen some of this pageant, even without modern aids like 10 x 40-power binoculars and 30-power spotting scopes. November in the year 1011 was surely also marked by "v" formations, geese calling constantly as flock after flock crossed the Ozarks, the Arkansas River Valley, and long green ridges of the Ouachita Mountains, toward their southern winter quarters.

Native Americans and the settlers of the 1830s witnessed flocks of Wood Ducks, American Wigeon, Gadwalls, Green-winged Teal, Mallards, Northern Pintail, Blue-winged Teal, and Northern Shovelers. Small flocks would have rested and fed around natural prairie wetlands and in backwaters and cut-off channels formed by big rivers.

People who lived in the valley of the Arkansas hunted waterfowl, especially in natural oxbows like Ned Lake and Hollis Lake east of Van Buren. Geese and puddle ducks gathered in the shallows of the Arkansas River along some sandy island where willows provided cover. The evidence for the past includes the bones of "greenhead" Mallards in numerous archeological middens associated with Native Americans.

What folks wouldn't have seen one thousand years, or even one hundred years ago, were many diving birds, like loons. From Canvasbacks to Ruddy Ducks, virtually the entire tribe of the diving ducks, upwards of fifteen species, would have been missing from western Arkansas. We would find few, if any, of a now common species like Lesser Scaup. Chances of finding a Common Merganser would approach zero.

This does not mean that during a nasty November storm migrating flocks of diving ducks wouldn't have touched down at least briefly on the Arkansas River, or some wide open part of the White or Poteau Rivers. A loon or two may have stopped over for a few days. But during big storms these rivers would not have provided more than temporary refuge. They were neither deep enough nor large enough in area to accommodate mixed-species flocks with thousands of individual birds.

If they stopped, it was brief, and then they moved on to the natural lakes of the Coastal Plain and the Gulf of Mexico.

Opportunities afforded birds and birders in 2011 in western Arkansas date to the 1920s and especially the Great Depression of the 1930s. The federal government provided folks out of other work with an honorable way to bring home a paycheck. People built lakes. Migrating birds eventually found them, and later, birders found the migrants.

William H. Deaderick of Hot Springs began to see new birds after Arkansas Light and Power Company constructed a dam on the Ouachita River forming Lake Catherine in 1924 and then a second dam in 1930 forming Lake Hamilton. He described it as follows: "a river length of twenty-four miles, a shoreline of 170 miles, and covers an area of 7,150 acres. The depth varies from wide shallows over the inundated flats to more than 100 feet in the river channel."

As early as 1935 he found what was then considered rare in Arkansas, a Common Loon, on Lake Hamilton. He followed this with another rarity, Horned Grebe. He also found and published notes for American White Pelican, Bufflehead, Red-breasted Merganser, Bald Eagle, Osprey, and Caspian Tern, all associated with new lakes.

Deaderick documented twenty-three significant records associated with the creation of these lakes. "The effect of recently impounded water on the water bird life of this section is shown by the addition of thirteen water birds to the state list, by the observation of four water birds of which there is only one previous record in the state, four of which there are only two previous records, and two recorded by only two observers." Many of the first Arkansas records were shorebirds like Piping Plover, Baird's Sandpiper, and Sanderling, and others like Franklin's Gull. He found them and most of the diving ducks with his 25-power telescope and 8-power binoculars.

William J. Baerg was making similar observations in the Ozark Mountains of northwestern Arkansas. As was the case in Deaderick's Ouachita Mountains, there were no natural lakes in the Arkansas Ozarks and no diving bird habitat at Fayetteville where Baerg taught entomology and ornithology at the University of Arkansas. The federal government was acquiring and rehabilitating abandoned and oftentimes eroding farmland, which eventually became part of the Ozark National

Forested Ozark hills rise above the inundated channel of the White River dammed to form Beaver Lake. The view here looks south from the mountains along Slate Gap Road, in December 2009.

Forest. Lake Wedington, which impounded 102 acres, was constructed twelve miles west of Fayetteville in 1938.

In his 1951 *Birds of Arkansas,* Baerg published numerous waterbird records for Lake Wedington for 1938–1939. He had sightings of Common Loon, Pied-billed Grebe, Redhead, Ring-necked Duck (which "occurred in considerable numbers"), Canvasback, Lesser Scaup (up to six hundred during the winter of 1938–1939), Common Goldeneye, Bufflehead, Hooded Merganser, Red-breasted Merganser, and Common Merganser.

These records were unique for the time. They foreshadowed what was to come, as more streams were dammed to create impoundments.

My Kennedy relatives lost their farm near Magazine in Logan County in 1929, during the Depression. Like many others in western Arkansas, they migrated to factory jobs in Fort Smith. My grandfather Ernest Kennedy worked in a factory that went out on strike. While the factory was closed, he got temporary work during construction of Lake Fort Smith (1935–1936). Men like him were loaded on flatbed trucks and hauled twenty-five miles to the dam site, all for two dollars a day.

Streams have been dammed all over northwestern Arkansas. The Civilian Conservation Corps began work on Shores Lake in the Ozark National Forest in the 1930s (82 acres). Lake Leatherwood at Eureka Springs is a product of the 1940s (85 acres). Lake Atalanta (35 acres) in Rogers was constructed in 1936.

Growing communities like Fayetteville eventually dammed everything available in the scramble to keep up with public-water supplies. Lake Fayetteville (194 acres) dates to 1949. This was soon inadequate, so the White River was dammed to create Lake Sequoyah in 1959 (495 acres). As a result of population growth and expansion in the poultry-processing industry, the White River was dammed again in 1966, forming Beaver Lake (40,463 acres).

Before Beaver Lake, the White River had been impounded in 1958 to form Table Rock Lake along the Arkansas-Missouri border (52,300 acres). A partial list of others includes Lake Elmdale near Springdale in 1953 (200 acres), Lake Hinkle near Waldron completed in 1971 (960 acres), and Lake Bob Kidd near Prairie Grove in 1975 (200 acres). Arkansas Game and Fish Commission initiated its lake construction program in 1945. Currently, there are 29 lakes totaling about 22,000 water acres, including several in northwestern Arkansas. The McClellan-Kerr Arkansas River Navigation System was completed in 1968. This has involved basically making the river into a giant lake.

Lakes large and small provide habitat for all kinds of ducks, grebes, loons, and gulls. Bald Eagles visit them all. Birds reported excitedly by Deaderick and Baerg have become commonplace on these lakes. Like eagles, birders visit them all.

Lake Fayetteville was out in the northwest Arkansas farm country when it was constructed in 1949. Today's public park dominated by trees was mostly open fields with big coveys of Northern Bobwhites. There were farms, but no subdivisions and no businesses. Busy highways did not ring the lake. The lake had mudflats attractive to migrating Greater Yellowlegs and other shorebirds in its early years. The Fayetteville Square was five miles south. Springdale was a similar distance north. The main highway through the area, U.S. 71, was a narrow, two-lane road. There were 88,000 people strung out along 71 between Fayetteville and Rogers in 1950.

Northwest Arkansas Mall was constructed on one of the pastures just southwest of Lake Fayetteville in 1972. By this time population had risen to 130,000. Fayetteville surged north and Springdale surged south. By the 1980s, Lake Fayetteville was crowded on all sides by an urban conglomeration that could be rightly called Northwest Arkansas City.

Today I can combine a check of Lake Fayetteville during the fall waterfowl migration with shopping. After checking the lake, I can knock out some Christmas shopping at Northwest Arkansas Mall and Walmart. Pushing a shopping cart, I ask myself, "Who am I?" I benefit from so many shopping opportunities. The binoculars and scope are in the trunk as I shop. When I'm done, out come the optics; to the trunk go shopping packages. Watching birds at the lake, I feel a little guilty about being such an active participant in our society's "shop 'til you drop" addiction.

By 2000, population in the area exceeded 311,000. Maybe it's 500,000 now. It's still a great place for birding. The following is from my field notes for a few days of the waterfowl migration during a big fall, 2003:

> November 6, 2003. Lake Fayetteville, 1–3 PM.
> We finally have fall type weather again. 80 degrees on Monday and Tuesday, but cooled off Tuesday late and by Wednesday it's cold. Rained last night and light rain, 40s, foggy today. Basically the entire world is a light mist. Went to the dam first: Common Loon-2; Pied-billed Grebe 5–6; Horned Grebe-2; Double-crested Cormorant-1; Flocks of Snow Geese flying over. Huge raft of ducks out in the mist, but I can't see them well. Here are my guesses about what's in the raft: about 800 birds including Mallard, Northern Shoveler (40+), Redhead, Ring-necked Duck, Lesser Scaup ~600; Bufflehead, Hooded Merganser, and Ruddy Duck (at least one group of 11). There's also a nice raft of American Coots ~120. Five Ring-billed Gulls fly over.
> It's just a huge mass of birds.

Mike Mlodinow and I were on the phone the night of November 6, strategizing about birding for the seventh. We need a plan that will maximize coverage of all these artificial lakes. Our plan will not include shopping at the mall. This looks like *the* big waterfowl day of the season. We plan to hit as many lakes as possible.

Temperatures go down into the 30s during the night, but

November 7 dawns a little clearer, alternating with mist or light rain. The cold front is still passing through—which means the birds are still passing through—which means the birding can be outstanding. I pick up Mike at 7:00 a.m., and by 7:30 we have spotting scopes scanning Bob Kidd Lake near Prairie Grove. My observations of big rafts of water birds at Lake Fayetteville the previous day turns out to be triply true at Bob Kidd. Here are more field notes:

> November 7, 2004. Bob Kidd Lake near Prairie Grove with Mike Mlodinow, 7:30–8:57 AM (rain):
>
> Common Loon-10; Pied-billed Grebe-7; Horned Grebe-2; American White Pelican-1; Double-crested Cormorant-3; Great Egret-5; Snow Goose-hundreds and heard flocks overhead that we couldn't see; Wood Duck-1 male; Gadwall-6; Green-winged Teal-4; Mallard-8; Northern Shoveler-71;
>
> Canvasback-7; Redhead-42; Ring-necked Duck-14; Greater Scaup-1 male; Lesser Scaup-1,500 (!) (actual number probably higher); Bufflehead-200; Hooded Merganser-4; Red-breasted Merganser-3; Ruddy Duck-360; Black Vulture-3; Turkey Vulture-27; Bald Eagle-1 adult; American Coot-56; Dunlin-5 (in flight); Ring-billed Gull-85; Franklin's Gull-1; American Pipits (50+).

With mist, rain, and fog closing in on Bob Kidd, we pack up the scopes and head for Lake Fayetteville. Conditions are still rough, but near the dam at Lake Fayetteville there is a covered pavilion used by fishermen. After visiting the dam, we head for the Lake Fayetteville Environmental Study Center dock, with views of the lake's middle section.

We walk carefully down the trail. We don't want to flush any water birds rafting near the dock. One misstep and the whole place will explode into a winged uproar. We creep, creep, creep down the trail, using bushes for cover, Then set up our scopes. WOW! The whole mid-lake area is FULL of waterfowl: certainly three to four thousand birds. And then, suddenly, the dreaded explosion: the biggest waterfowl concentration of the season flushes in an instant in a vast, vast roar of wings.

It's not us, but the boat from Lake Fayetteville Environmental Study Center hauling students out to see waterfowl. I have this sinking feeling we have probably missed the best of the best, in terms of fall waterfowl migration. And yet—there are still birds as the boat passes by. And, just as good, the students got to see it well.

Gulls at Tontitown, west of Springdale on March 14, 2011, including Lesser Black-backed, Herring, and Ring-billed. Most are Ring-billed Gulls, fairly common all winter in western Arkansas.

More field notes:

November 7, 2003. Lake Fayetteville 10–11:30 AM, with Mike Mlodinow:

Common Loon-12, plus a mystery flock of 8 loons that flew over us with 7 birds of one size, and 1 bird slightly larger? Pied-billed Grebe-10; Horned Grebe-5; Double-crested Cormorant-several; Great Blue Heron; Snow Goose-300; American Wigeon-6; Gadwall-100; Green-winged Teal-4; Mallard-5; Northern Shoveler-10; Canvasback-12; Redhead-20; Ring-necked Duck-20; Greater Scaup-1 female; Lesser Scaup-200 (I was just counting them through a crack in the bushes when they were flushed, so number was higher); Bufflehead-100; Hooded Merganser-2; Red-breasted Merganser-1 female; Ruddy Duck-1,200 (!) (ignored the boat I guess); Turkey Vulture-5; American Coot-100; Ring-billed Gull-2+.

The rain slows and we return to Bob Kidd for additional observations of that Western Grebe–type bird. There's no doubt it's an *Aechmophorus* grebe, and most likely correctly identified as Western Grebe

A. occidentalis. Mike is concerned that with rain, mist and distance across the lake, it might actually be Clark's Grebe, *A. clarkii.* That would be a first state record. We settle on Western Grebe, then head north, to the state fish hatchery at Centerton in Benton County.

The hatchery doesn't have deep water like Lake Fayetteville and Bob Kidd, but it is still a large area with big open ponds that have proven attractive to waterfowl. Plus, it has the best dependable mudflat habitat.

More field notes:

> November 7, 2003. Craig State Fish Hatchery 2:59–3:59 PM, with Mike Mlodinow:
>
> Double-crested Cormorant-1; Osprey-1; Great Blue Heron-4; Great Egret-7; American Wigeon-4; Gadwall-200; Green-winged Teal; Mallard-120; Northern Pintail-4; Blue-winged Teal-5; Northern Shoveler-50; Ring-necked Duck-31; Lesser Scaup-25; Bufflehead-5; Ruddy Duck-5; American Coot-85; Killdeer-16; Least Sandpiper-8; Dunlin-17; Wilson's Snipe-20; Ring-billed Gull-15; Vesper Sparrow; Savannah Sparrow-25; American Pipit-2. "Thus ends an incredible day."

There would have been no such big days of waterfowling like November 6–7, 2003, prior to damming Clear Creek for Lake Fayetteville, Bob Kidd Creek for Bob Kidd Lake, prior to digging shallow ponds and damming an artesian spring at Centerton, prior to Lake Fort Smith and Wedington. No doubt, a big November front and its accompanying bird migration would have been interesting here, even before the 1930s, but it would have been different.

In more than twenty years, Mike Mlodinow and I have never gone to the Buffalo River in the second week of November. Unlike most rivers in our region, the Buffalo River has not been buried under a big lake. Despite the river's deserved reputation for scenic beauty, it's not our November hotspot. Tens of thousands of folks in Texas and Louisiana may plan their entire vacations around the chance for a few days of fantastic canoeing on a natural untamed river, but Western Grebes do not know the Buffalo River. In short, the Buffalo National River is NOT the place to study fall waterfowl migration. The river's 145 canoeable miles is of the very highest ecological value, but it is also of no value if what you seek is Canvasbacks.

To create habitat for loons, Western Grebes, and Surf Scoters, we

Mike Mlodinow in the field at Woolsey Wet Prairie in Fayetteville on October 23, 2011. On the previous day he identified Cassin's Sparrow there, the first time this western bird has even been seen in the Ozarks.

bury natural places like the Buffalo River that work best for Wood Ducks and Louisiana Waterthrushes. To get good habitat for a big waterfowl day in November, you substitute seasonal ebbs and flows of natural rivers for deep, cold, stable reservoirs. You bury smooth, colorful cobbles and gravel bars of sandstone and limestone. You bury the noisy riffles of a flowing river. You bury the water willow, witch hazel, and alder. You bury the chance to see a flock of Pine Siskins probing the alders for tiny seeds.

In creating big lakes, you bury all traces of prior civilization. In return, you have a sizeable expanse of water big enough to accommodate ski boats and party barges, and a flock of American White Pelicans. You get an ecosystem where a gizzard shad die-off can bring out a flock of two hundred Ring-billed Gulls, with maybe a Herring Gull or two mixed in. You get a place where folks with speedboats can race across

Northwest Arkansas Audubon Society field trip to Lake Fayetteville on November 15, 2009. Left to right across the front are some of the region's most active birders, including Mike Mlodinow (bins up), Joanie Patterson, Michelle Viney (bins up), Jacque Brown, David Oakley, and H. David Chapman.

two miles of flat water propelled by an engine suitable for a jet fighter. You get a place for building vacation homes. You get a stable water supply to allow towns to provide clean water for homes and for factories to create jobs. And yes, you get a place to set up spotting scopes and tripods.

Welcome, welcome to the birder's Disney World. These places are as phony as a three-dollar bill, funhouses for big kids with binoculars and spotting scopes—expensive toys. And yet, as I see Common Goldeneyes in flight, all black and white, wings whirling, racing low across endless ranks of low waves, it doesn't seem to matter overly much that natural forces didn't see fit to create for us a bunch of lakes and ponds in western Arkansas.

People built the lakes for their own purposes because they are restless for a better life. They want a dependable August water supply. People in such circumstances are not overly concerned about the natural values of a free-flowing Buffalo. But people were also the ones who said "No" to plans to dam the Buffalo River, said "Yes" to keeping it wild and free-flowing. Maybe not the same people, but people anyway. The needs of people manifest in a bewildering variety of ways across vast times and cultures. These manifestations include rivers preserved as well as rivers killed and their bodies buried under cold-water reservoirs.

I sit home with my field notes and puzzle over the ambiguity. I object to the destruction of natural streams caused by dams. I celebrate the loon that finds this former stream, now lake, during its migration.

Damn those people who build dams and could care less about natural rivers. I laugh at myself aloud, in my bedroom, at the contradictions manifest in my own life. Look at my nice big spotting scope and its sturdy tripod—good for nothing but a windy winter day on a big phony reservoir. Damn the people who destroyed the White River, the old Arkansas River, and Clear Creek.

Why isn't the earth good enough as we find it? "Treat the earth well," goes an old proverb ascribed to Native Americans. "It was not given to you by your parents, it was loaned to you by your children."

We've had global warming weather, or at least a long warm fall. It was seventy-eight degrees here just two days ago, and no frost yet. But during the last two days, November 6–7, the Great North sends down her gifts of birds. All the tribes of waterfowl are headed our way. Despite damming most every river in the Ozarks, there seems not yet enough such artificial water to hold them all.

When we approach November and the annual waterfowl migration, I always remember one now departed who loved ducks and duck hunting. I want you to meet my friend Charlie.

Charlie McCrary was born in 1909 in Homer, northwestern Louisiana. His boyhood playgrounds included the winding path of Bayou D'Arbonne—creeks, natural oxbow lakes, and sloughs. Like many kids in the southern pines and swamps, he grew up with a strong attachment to self-reliance, double-barreled shotgun in hand. Charlie and his spouse Ruby Tugwell settled in a country of upland pine and the low-lying swamps along the lower Ouachita River near Huttig, in Union County, Arkansas. Like Bayou D'Arbonne, the lower Ouachita River landscape is formed by meandering creeks, oxbows, and upland pine: millions of acres of loblolly and shortleaf pines.

Charlie had deep set, clear blue eyes, a meditative look, expressive hands. He was valedictorian at Huttig High School in 1930, then made a career in the Union County sawmills. His millwright's reputation was earned by problem solving and quick thinking that kept a mill operating. Off the job he was on the Huttig School Board, helped establish the infrastructure for safe drinking water in the community, was a song leader in the Baptist Church. Have I forgotten to add hunting and fishing?

Ruby taught school for families of the mill hands and gave music lessons in the home. They had a daughter, Patty, who eventually went to college and settled in Fayetteville, with her husband, Bob Besom. It was through them that I met Charlie.

During those years I was helping in an effort to study and hopefully save endangered Red-cockaded Woodpeckers. Union County had once been a Red-cockaded stronghold, at least before the big mills were established. Red-cockadeds had evolved a lifestyle that required huge, older living pines for their roost and nest cavities. These same trees frequently went to Charlie's mill. It was the parents of Ruby's students who sawed the trees and operated the mill, which sawed the boards from trees where the woodpeckers had lived.

So it was woodpecker business that brought me into Union County and through Patty, to the wide, comfortable porch of a weathered, framed, tin-roofed home where her folks lived. There was dense humidity of a south Arkansas summer. From the big-pine shade a single Summer Tanager gave its *p-tuck, p-tuck* calls. There was Patty's old swing in the yard, and an old flatboat pulled up behind the house, not far from the Ouachita River. I was to hear that day the first of Charlie's many adventures in the swamp woods of northern Louisiana and southern Arkansas.

Charlie knew deep-river catfish with enormous whiskers, had spent a stormy night in a hollow tree with—well, who knows what was in there with him? He marveled at the big cottonmouth snakes. He told about a buck deer of mighty local reputation in the shady deep woods. He recalled the Mallard he shot and presumed dead that escaped Lazarus-like back to the wilds. He recalled sleety fall days with long open stretches of the lower Ouachita bursting at the seams with migrating ducks and geese.

My first knowledge of canned Mallards originated from that trip. Where I grew up, we had canned green beans, but no ducks. Charlie shot the ducks. Ruby did the canning in quart Mason jars.

A male and female Mallard at Lake Atalanta in Rogers on November 18, 2010.

As the McCrarys aged, the plan was for Charlie and Ruby to retire in Fayetteville. The lower Ouachita swarmed with Wood Ducks and catfish, but not many doctors or services for folks in their eighties. Patty and Bob loved their trips to south Arkansas, but they could better care for Charlie and Ruby in their large, comfortable, old-fashioned home in Fayetteville.

I saw Charlie off and on at the Besoms' in Fayetteville. He told many stories during these visits. Typically, he sat in an old rocker moved from his home in Union County. Near the rocker was a magnifying glass, the monthly hometown newspaper, a family photo album, and the Bible. The setting for one of my favorite stories is in the hard times of the Depression years.

"We were out of work at the mill," Charlie starts. "The mill owner was having a holiday party and needed ducks for his out-of-town guests. I had only four shells. Shells were high then. Every one counted. Boy, shells were dear in those days.

"I knew right where those ducks would go—a big fall flock of Wood Ducks would be in that back slough fattening on acorns. It was a good acorn year. Maybe they were planning to roost there. I had to walk in there two miles, but I knew it was the best place.

"I was hiding behind a cypress snag when here they came,

swimming and feeding. Right there, just like I thought! Boy, I could hardly breathe!"

Charlie's hands come up from the rocker's arms, imaginatively cradling the old double-barrel. His blue eyes squint slightly, very slightly down the shotgun barrel, finger light on the trigger.

"The ducks spun around on that dark water. Then they spun back, slowly swimming away. I knew they'd seen me, or just maybe caught a little movement from my breathing. They flushed! Nothing but Wood Ducks in the air!"

Charlie rises slightly from the rocker. The ducks are right there with us, in the room, in Fayetteville, headed back up the river. The females call *oo-eee, oo-eee*. Up goes his shotgun. BOOM! BOOM! Booming rolls down through the old back swamp. BOOM! BOOM! Shotgun blasts echo through the Besom home.

Twelve Wood Ducks eventually fall. Back he goes through the bottomland woods, two miles with twelve ducks. These he swaps at the mill store for a new complete box of shells—enough with care to tide him over until there was more work at the mill.

Ruby passed first. Charlie was ninety-three when he died in 2002. He was hospitalized the last few weeks. I made it up to see him and took along my laptop with bird images from around western Arkansas.

At my Mallard images he performs the rapid *quack, quack, quack* with great enthusiasm. He knows up close and personal that it's the hen Mallard who quacks when the flock startles into sudden flight. Once again, Mallards head in wild synchronous flight up the Ouachita, through cypress swamps and hardwood bottomlands, into open sky, completely free of time.

Woodpecker Business

I WAS HIRED to help trap and band Red-cockaded Woodpeckers, *Picoides borealis*, in 1980. RCW is what we call them in the business. It's eight and one-half-inches long with a black-and-white barred back and pronounced white cheek patch. Tiny red tufts on the male's head are seen only if you are very lucky. Its rarity is of recent, and now well-understood, origin.

Professor Douglas James of the University of Arkansas–Fayetteville had obtained funds to study RCWs in the late 1970s. Dennis Hart was one of Doug's grad students. Helping Dennis with his thesis fieldwork was my first job in the woodpecker business.

Our study site was near Crossett along the Arkansas-Louisiana border. The Corps of Engineers had just finished a dam across the lower Ouachita River near Crossett on the Louisiana line. Part of this Ouachita–Black River Navigation Project included creation of Felsenthal National Wildlife Refuge and management of ten thousand acres of pinelands with RCWs.

For several humid July weeks we watch woodpeckers early mornings and late evenings near their roost trees, which are covered with shiny resinous pitch. The pitch flows when they peck through bark into living sapwood. By 8:00 p.m. the sun is setting and shadows creep up the pines. Entrances to natural cavities where the birds roost slowly darken. Suddenly, with excited calls and great elan, woodpeckers sweep in among the cavity trees, perch briefly, fly away, then back, then head off to visit nearby trees.

They chatter loudly and chase one another in spirals up the trunks. They perch on pines and flake away bark exposing hidden ants and beetles. They peck at resin wells. One by one, they disperse to individual trees. With stiff tail feathers propped against the sap-covered bark, they

An adult male Red-cockaded Woodpecker moved to the Ouachita National Forest as part of population recovery efforts in 2001.

perched at cavity entrances, look in, look out, then push into the holes. Silence falls over the cluster of trees. We set traps over cavity entrances.

We are out by 5:30 a.m. the following morning midst rhythmic singing of Chuck-will's-widows. The sun's rays become quietly visible through pine needles. Pine Warblers sing their high trills in the treetops. Suddenly, woodpeckers exit their holes. Again, there is much *yack*ing and general excitement. Hopefully, we've got one of them in a trap.

We're finished by 6:30 a.m. By then, Highway 82 roars with trucks hauling pine logs to Crossett's mills. The local economy has revolved around logging since at least 1901, when Crossett Lumber Company laid out a town, population 2,500 by 1907. Logging and milling pines has been big business all over the South since after the Civil War.

Working with this bird means working with logging. Like my dad used to say, it's how the cow eats the cabbage.

Doug James has also obtained grant money for a statewide RCW survey. After trapping and banding at Felsenthal, we obtain permission to search for woodpeckers on privately owned timberland in Ashley and Union Counties. Historically, this was Arkansas's RCW stronghold. The companies sought compliance with the Endangered Species Act by not cutting obvious roost trees.

Logged areas have regenerated as jungle—a growed-up mess, as a friend puts it where a machete is *de rigueur*. The technique of marking trees with broad bands of red paint has worked. We find many marked trees, but few still have RCWs. We estimate the woodpecker population has plummeted in this locale by 85–90 percent in ten years.

The company refuses permission for further searches. Maybe they think we have manipulated data to embarrass them? Eventually, a forester explains. "Red-cockaded Woodpeckers don't pay their own bills. Providing them with suitable habitat reduces the amount of marketable timber." He is not saying this out of disrespect. Saving their roost trees was considered reasonable management.

Our results, plus those elsewhere in the South, suggest that saving individual trees isn't enough.

The southern Arkansas woodpecker country is a six-hour drive from Fayetteville. However, there is a population two hours south of Fayetteville, in the Ouachita Mountains. Welcome to Scott County, 70 percent of which is Ouachita National Forest. My mother's Kennedy family immigrated into the Ouachitas after the Civil War. They eventually settled in Lick Creek valley, near the modern community of Magazine, in Logan County, adjacent Scott County. As is the case throughout the Ouachitas, Lick Creek drains a long narrow valley ringed by pine-clad ridges. The only farmable soil is in the valley. I assume Kennedys cut pines. Even if they weren't birders, I figure they probably recognized the RCW's pitch-covered trees.

In sheer mass, shortleaf pines have provided the Ouachita Mountains a significant source of economic power for more than a century. In the early 1900s, it was termed the "Greatest shortleaf pine forest in the world." This was the country my mother's family knew. This virgin pine forest was cut and sent to mills primarily during the years from 1900 to 1950.

Logging booms like the one that swept the Ouachitas altogether consumed 200 million acres of various pines in the southeastern United

States. In less than a century, 99 percent of the original virgin pine forests disappeared. Milled pine timber was hauled by railroads all over the country. This included timbers for the home in which my mother was born in Logan County, my father's in Crawford County, and the home in which I grew up in Fort Smith.

A few RCWs held on in the Ouachitas. I saw my first Ouachita woodpeckers in the early 1980s at an Arkansas Audubon Society meeting. Biologist Warren Montague, of the Poteau Ranger District, at Waldron—two hours south of Fayetteville—showed me more woodpeckers in the late 1980s.

My mother was then living in Booneville, not far from where she was born and only thirty minutes from Waldron. Her health was declining. I was working at the University of Arkansas–Fayetteville and making numerous trips to Booneville. She told me stories about the old Kennedys. She took me to Lick Creek Cemetery, well stocked with Kennedys and related families, like the Van Allens and Hokits. She showed me the old home place and a barn that was built by my Kennedy grandfather.

In her voice and memories were the pine-clad ridges and narrow valleys of the Ouachitas. Now these voices were calling me, too.

Warren Montague and I worked together on an RCW survey that covered all the data we could find for 1975 to 1990. We were able to document the historical presence of at least forty-one and probably more RCW clusters on the National Forest and on private timberlands in western Arkansas.

Unfortunately, data were similar in certain respects to what Doug James and I found concerning private lands in southern Arkansas. Only about one-third of the known woodpecker clusters on the Ouachita National Forest were still active in 1990. None remained on private lands. Recommended techniques approved by the U.S. Fish and Wildlife Service had been employed. Nevertheless, some formerly active clusters had become "bulges" surrounded on several sides by clear cuts.

In the fall of 1990, the Forest Service offered me financial support for a master of science degree. Upon successful completion, I would have a permanent job, part of which would involve helping Warren and others with woodpecker recovery.

Joe Neal and Ariel Neal during annual Kid's Fishing Derby at Truman Baker Lake south of Waldron, June 12, 1993. *Photographer unknown.*

    I had many doubts about the other roles that would come with this opportunity. I was recently divorced. My former spouse and I were cooperating in rearing our five-year-old daughter, Ariel, in Fayetteville. How could this arrangement possibly work if I was away in Waldron? My seventy-year-old mother lived in Booneville, near where I would be stationed in Waldron. While trying to start a Forest Service career at midlife, I would be part-time father, part-time caregiver.

    I found an old page from a Neal family Bible that showed one of my relatives was part of the Bates clan of Scott County. Therefore, despite fears of so great a change, I comforted myself with the thought that graduate school and the Forest Service would be a homecoming of sorts.

In 1989, the Ouachita National Forest plans to capture and band thirty-two adult woodpeckers in thirteen cavity tree clusters with active trees. This will be the initial step in rebuilding the Ouachita population.

Beginning in February 1990, trapping teams consist of Forest Service personnel, plus folks from the University of Arkansas–Fayetteville, Arkansas Audubon Society, and Arkansas Natural Heritage Commission. John McLemore from the Forest Supervisor's office in Hot Springs provides me on-the-job training with light-weight Swedish climbing ladders we use to reach woodpecker cavities.

Our U of A trapping team is assigned to catch a bird in a cavity about forty-five feet high in a tree with a bright orange number 1. The cluster of pines is at the end of a rough trail above Buffalo Creek south of Waldron. We observe the bird as it roosts in the evening. We adjust the pole and trap to match the height of the cavity.

The motel alarm in Waldron goes off at 4:00 a.m. I am behind the wheel as we drive in at 4:30 a.m. Nothing, and I mean absolutely nothing, looks familiar. The ridge trail seems too long. Turns are not in remembered directions. Trees and shadows loom at odd angles, appearing suddenly and disconcertingly in the predawn darkness. I think I'm hallucinating. Was I really here yesterday? Did I miss a turn? Finally, something looks familiar, but the woodpecker trees seem out-of-place. Where is the number 1 tree?

Even with a strong flashlight, the cavity entrance is all-but-invisible. Is that a knot in the tree, or the cavity? Weren't there two holes? Why didn't we notice this last night? I see first light in the east. Are we too late? We lift the pole with trap, up, up. The trap sways, slightly grazing the tree. A dark form darts out suddenly. All we hear is wing beats and a muffled woodpecker chirp, then silence: we've missed. We'll be back tomorrow.

Nothing looked familiar, either, as I started graduate school in fall 1990. It was like the long ridge road up to number 1 tree. Trying to get back to the academic life left me with feelings not unlike missing a bird in early morning darkness. Everything in life seemed out of place and upside down: odd, shadowy forms in darkness.

There was a research proposal to prepare. What would justify the Forest Service supporting my master's degree? It would involve woodpeckers, but how? What? Shouldn't I just drop this? As I struggled with these questions on campus, Warren Montague and wildlife tech Keith Piles had already started answering questions at Waldron.

The virgin Ouachita forest had been extensively logged. What became National Forest was a second-growth forest, with scattered older relics of the virgin forest. Woodpeckers that survived the first cuttings preferred older relics for their cavity excavations, but relics were too few and far between to stimulate population growth. They needed a temporary fix, a bridge. That's what Warren and Keith were doing: building a bridge.

Keith manufactured artificial woodpecker cavities at the Forest Service work center in Waldron. First he cut a block of western red cedar about shoebox size. Within this block he drilled a cavity about the size of a tennis ball canister. In the field, they used chainsaws to cut holes in suitable pines. They secured the block firmly with wedges and wood filler. In two years, they installed an initial 120 of these artificial cavities within the existing woodpecker clusters and elsewhere to support population growth.

Meanwhile, back in Fayetteville, I presented a seminar on the woodpecker situation at Waldron. Fellow grad student Patty Moore asked, "Do you see snakes on the trees?" She had used plastic garden netting to trap snakes attempting to climb trees where Acorn Woodpeckers nest in California. Could one of the problems in the Ouachitas involve tree-climbing snakes attempting to eat nestling woodpeckers?

In May 1991, I finished my first year of course work. A summer of woodpecker nesting was just ahead. Jim Johnson of the Arkansas Coop Unit handed me the keys of a new Suburban. It was a lovely May afternoon as I left the university campus. My feelings about the day were mixed. An experiment to potentially quantify snake climbing on woodpecker trees (and hence, impacts of snakes on woodpecker nesting) seemed a long shot. This would require a trip to the hardware store for a roll of plastic garden netting.

Besides snakes, I was thinking about my family. My mother was looking forward to me being in the Waldron-Booneville area. Ariel, who was six, would be fine spending more time with her mother while I was gone, but I would miss her.

Emotionally, I was already out in the Ouachita pine forests. While my mind was spinning, the Suburban plowed into the back of a Chevy

Blazer near Ace Hardware, four blocks off campus. The only injury was a flood of paperwork.

※ ※ ※

In summer heat, volatile essential oils in pinesap send the fresh scent of turpentine wafting through the Ouachitas. Old timers tapped the best sap trees for resins that would then be distilled into turpentine. They noticed that certain chatty birds with bold white cheek patches also found these turpentine trees.

Now I too become familiar with turpentine trees. On a daily basis, we check woodpecker nests and roost cavities, mostly fifteen to forty-five feet from the ground. We reach the cavities via Swedish climbing ladders, chained tightly against sappy pine trees. We are the new "turpentine hands" for sure: sappy hands, sappy gloves, sap dripping on us from the trunk above.

It's the woodpeckers that peck through the bark into sapwood, releasing flows of sticky, aromatic oleoresin. Repeated pecking sends resins down the tree trunk in long flows, like candle wax. This is not recreational pecking. Rat snakes are expert tree climbers. A high percentage of their summer diet consists of birds. To eat woodpeckers, the snakes must avoid pinesap. It has been shown experimentally that they writhe and even drop from trees as their belly scales contact fresh resins.

Snake questions increasingly dominate my two field seasons as a graduate student. With help from biologist Frances Rothwein, plus Warren and Keith, I attach skirts of plastic garden netting on active woodpecker trees. The skirt will hopefully trap snakes climbing from the ground. Doug James suggests that I also skirt trees of a similar size, but lacking woodpecker cavities. This serves as an experimental control. Is snake climbing random, or aimed at specific trees?

Constant, repetitive *churr-churr-churr* begging calls of nestling woodpeckers are easy to hear, even at distance from the tree. Do snakes hear this? We band nestlings and return in following weeks to check the brood's progress. One nest is in a sappy pine about thirty feet from the ground. We expect to hear begging calls from three chicks banded in the week before. We are greeted, not by *churrs,* but silence. The sole nest occupant is a black rat snake.

Wildlife Technician Keith Piles with a rat snake that consumed nestlings in a Red-cockaded Woodpecker cavity tree in the Ouachita NF, June 2005.

We do not trap rat snakes on any control trees. This supports the theory that rat snakes do not randomly climb pines during the nesting season. Climbing occurs primarily when the brood consists of older nestlings. In short, the rat snakes know where they are going. We never had reason to doubt that the pine resin barrier was the key natural defense against rat snakes. However, snakes were capable of avoiding this barrier, at least sometimes.

In biology, issues aren't couched as good versus evil; that's religion. From an ecosystem perspective, rat snakes are interesting predators and aren't the enemy of good land management. Their role in the ecosystem is complex, like that of birds, insects, and forces like fire—and people, of course. But for now, with RCWs so rare, rat snakes must dine elsewhere.

For a few years I rented an old farmhouse five miles east of Waldron. It was typical: wood frame, painted white, screened porch, bathroom added when flush toilets came into vogue in the 1950s. The old place was slowly sinking into the native soil of western Arkansas.

A country house of this kind starts as a dream, usually of newlyweds. There's a plan and a building site, then comes a family. Later, if farming is productive, or if jobs are available in town, a new and better-built house is constructed nearby. The original becomes a "budding house" because newlywed offspring make their first home and hopefully conceive the first grandchildren there. Finally, it may become a rent house after the children are all budded-off.

Ule and Jean Horn owned the budding house I rented. They were retired from careers on the farm and with the Waldron public schools. She was a cook, he a maintenance man. Jean was not retired from vegetable gardening, quilt making, and grandchild rearing. Ule was not retired from horses, deer hunting, and unnamed farm chores, especially putting up hay in late summer. I met them when they were in their late seventies. The Horns, horses, dogs, and grandchildren seemed to find in me an acceptable neighbor.

Strange things happened to me there. Small items just disappeared. I returned to Fayetteville every week, sometimes for as much as five days. When I got back, my toothbrush might be gone. Another time it was a flashlight battery and a spoon. I had pictures of my daughter Ariel on the table. One, but not all, of these disappeared. My girlfriend left red hair barrettes during one of her visits—these disappeared. A plastic thimble from my mother's sewing box—left open in the living room—gone.

It might be dismissed as absent mindedness. After all, I was busy woodpeckering, with little time to lounge in the old house. But was I dealing with pilfering children during my absence? It was a country house after all and an old one to boot. Locks on doors and windows were mostly for show. But Ule and Jean never saw anyone around the house while I was in Fayetteville.

A vexing mystery it was, but the loss of barrettes, for example, was nothing compared with other unseen visitors. I'd heard growling and clawing under the house during otherwise quiet winter nights. These sounds were a source of wonder to me, alone in the old house. I enjoyed them until the night of what I thought was a fire.

I was snug under a big sleeping bag one February when I was suddenly awakened by an acrid smell. Was the old wiring in the house on fire? Startled awake, I ran for the door and stood outside, freezing in my underwear. There were no flames. The old house seemed as before, except as I became fully awake, I realized the acrid smell was associated with one of my unseen under-the-house visitors, a striped skunk. The whole house was skunked-up. It took weeks to air out. I went to work skunky.

Now I know why country people keep numerous dogs. It's not just that they bark at strangers. They don't like skunks. I had no dogs down at the budding house. Ule trapped nine skunks from under the house.

Late winter and early spring is not just about skunks. During warm spells frogs began to sing at farm ponds. I opened the windows to enjoy them—and also to continue the process of airing the house from skunk night. It seemed the Ouachitas had billions of tiny spring peepers, vast choruses filling the nights with high-pitched and high-spirited calls. Along with the peepers I heard low, deep, sonorous, and occasionally explosive calls. Peepers sang soprano. Who sang basso?

I had occasional visitors from the University of Arkansas in Fayetteville. Doug James made a trip down with a new graduate student, Jeff Briggler. Jeff and Doug soon solved the mystery. I had crawfish frogs, an unusual creature in Arkansas, but fairly common around ponds in the old former prairie grasslands of Scott County.

The vast changes that have so remade the Arkansas landscape have been slower in the Waldron area. There are small farms with old frame or native stone homes. These farms include fields of various sizes with scattered ponds and woodlots. There are unpretentious country churches and traditional graveyards. Gravel roads leave the formal pavement and head into the backcountry in a refreshing and mysterious way.

Fields of cattle and chicken houses form a patchwork quilt separated by dense fencerows including cedars, winged elms, shortleaf pines, water oaks, all braided together by thickets of blackberries and greenbrier. I could hear Painted Buntings singing from fencerows across from the budding house. One day a fine male sang atop an old cedar

The greatest shortleaf pine forest in the world—the Ouachita National Forest in the Ouachita Mountains, looking south from within a cluster of Red-cockaded Woodpecker cavity trees on the Cold Springs Ranger District in western Arkansas.

in the front yard. I had a great rarity here, or so I thought, until I met a local birder, Ron Goddard.

Ron taught biology and ecology at Waldron High School and also drove a school bus. He grew up in the Scott County backcountry. There are Painteds all along these roads he told me. He'd counted seventeen in one afternoon. I would learn that his bus route was the rule rather than the exception when it came to Painted Buntings. With its patchwork quilt of fields and fencerows, rural Scott County is a stronghold for the somewhat mysterious Painted Bunting.

As for that other mystery involving disappearing barrettes, pictures, and thimbles: I got all my stuff back. One night I turned on a light and saw a pack rat apparently surveying what was left of my stuff. I followed it back to the bathroom, through a heater closet, and there found its treasure trove.

Atop Poteau Mountain, some forty miles south of Fort Smith, visitors pull off at lookouts and gaze south into the heart of the Ouachitas.

The valley of the Poteau River is there, and beyond, ridge after forested ridge, south to the mighty Fourche and Rich Mountains. One could seemingly glimpse beyond to the Gulf of Mexico.

From December through early April, the scene is enlivened by fire. Puffs of smoke rise above lofty pines and hardwoods. Like hats and hairdos, fires and smokes come in various shapes and sizes. Many puffs of smoke in the Ouachita National Forest rise from planned fires. But fire was no stranger in the historical Ouachitas. From the 1820s on, settlers routinely burned the forest to stimulate growth of grasses and other plants beneficial to wildlife and livestock. So did the Native Americans before them.

Under natural conditions, pine seedlings thrived in full sun where wildfire burned holes of various sizes in the forest. Prescribed fire also reduces loads of leaf and needle litter, limbs, and other combustibles that make young stands of trees subject to devastation in a wildfire. It prepares the landscape to support Red-cockaded Woodpeckers and numerous associated plants and animals.

In the 1980s, and into the early 1990s, it was more or less settled policy that very small, declining RCW populations, like the one in the Ouachita NF, were basically beyond hope and that limited resources available to save the bird from extinction ought to be spent saving and building a few large populations. That is, the Ouachita NF woodpeckers were to be written-off. But Warren Montague, and others of like mind, didn't see it that way. He didn't really care that the prevailing opinion was against him. He figured every population was worth saving, and anyone who really cared would find a way to get the job done.

On the Ouachita, Forest Service managers like Larry Hedrick and George Bukenhofer worked with Warren to set up special areas in which healthy pine-forest habitat would be restored. It would be possible to use thinning harvests to provide open conditions and prescribed burning to keep it open, as in the past. It was termed the Pine-Bluestem Project, for shortleaf pine and several species of native bluestem grasses.

As elsewhere in the South, habitat where RCWs were hanging on typically comprised the finest pine-timber producing country. Loggers, mill owners, and their representatives came warily to public meetings where the Pine-Bluestem Project was presented. It had not been that long since the rancorous Spotted Owl fight in the Pacific Northwest.

Loggers naturally assumed special effort for an endangered bird could put them out of work.

Environmentalists wanted more effort on behalf of endangered birds, but they distrusted using logging and prescribed burning in the habitat-restoration process. In the background of such distrust were potential lawsuits aimed at stopping all logging and prescribed burning.

The project eventually generated common ground. The tough issues were resolved by 1996. Most loggers came away satisfied mills would not close because of woodpeckers. Logging would continue, but it would be directed by biological needs of the woodpecker. Most environmentalists warily supported the plan. Thinning harvests would leave a canopy across the landscape. They had problems with so much burning but found it hard to argue that it wasn't necessary, at some level, for the woodpeckers.

Larry, George, and Warren are all experienced, determined people. But is determination enough? Could the Ouachita population of RCWs be rebuilt?

In 1990, we banded thirty-two adult birds in thirteen nests sites. The number of adult birds remained about the same for several years, and then declined as did the number of nesting attempts, and few juveniles were produced. These were all indications that the Ouachitas had a crashing population with mainly aging birds well past their prime in terms of nesting.

Young RCWs could be moved in from other larger populations, especially in Texas and Louisiana, giving a shot in the arm to the aging breeding population in the Ouachitas. Is determination enough?

"Determination" is a good descriptor for Warren G. Montague. He is tall with long legs, arms, and fingers, and a character to match his frame. His lunch bucket is an old type, held together with duck tape, reapplied as necessary to keep it in one piece as it bounces around in a work truck during woodpecker work. The bucket's contents have varied very little over the years. Start with the sandwich—it's jalapeño baloney, whenever he can find it. He once claimed he had a freezer full of this special baloney, a bulwark against the day when the company stopped making it. To the sandwich add a jar of chocolate milk. Joining jalapeño baloney and chocolate milk is a Snickers bar. And last, a banana—and no ordinary

Red-cockaded Woodpeckers are their business. Some Forest Service personnel working on the Ouachita National Forest including Warren Montague (left, without cap), Jason Nolde, Keith Piles, and Dan Brown, in Warren's office at Waldron, Arkansas, in May 2005.

banana, no green banana—a very well-ripened banana with black spots. In season, Warren may add a ripe tomato to the lunch line-up.

But what's this got to do with woodpeckers? One can assume that a person who sticks so religiously to a lunch menu is a person who knows what he likes, and what he doesn't like—a person with pretty settled opinions. That assumption would be correct—or as my brother-in-law would put it, "Roger that."

There's an illustrative story that dates back to Warren's early years in the Forest Service. Every year during the western fire season, FS crews from the Ouachita would go out west together on a chartered bus: a bunch of mostly young men together twenty-four hours a day. Pranks, jokes, and general rowdiness helped pass the time. Smoking was common among these crews, and Poteau Ranger District crew included smokers mostly crowded in the back of the bus. A nonsmoker, Warren chose the front of the bus to get as far away as he could from the smoke and ruckus. Since he was fairly new on the job and flagrantly separating himself, some of his fellow fire crew members decided he needed breaking in. The cowboy chosen for this ride was Harold Johnson.

So imagine the scene now. Warren is irritated by the smoke, and his coworkers have decided to gang up on him. Harold slips up the isle with a full load of smoke, piles down beside Warren, and blows a smoke ring directly into his face. So the joke's on Warren, right? Warren, 6 foot 2, turns on Harold, 5 foot 7, wraps his long fingers around Harold's neck and pushes him out of the seat. This is now fondly called the "neck stretch."

I almost got my neck stretched one day. It was in early 1994, right after President Clinton had signed into law the Brady Handgun Violence Prevention Act. The law, named for James Brady—wounded during an attempt on President Reagan's life in 1981—was considered a reasonable limitation on gun ownership around the U of A campus, and I held that view, too, though it was not a pressing issue to me. I just assumed most people supported it. I didn't know anyone who was a member of the National Rifle Association, or who thought the Brady Bill was an unconstitutional infringement on the second amendment to the U.S. constitution.

So Warren, Keith Piles, and I are belted into the front seat of our woodpecker work truck, headed for the Kisatchie National Forest in Texas to trap RCWs. We will then transport the birds we trap back to the Ouachita National Forest, where they will help to rebuild our population. Translocation it's called, and it's a key element in the effort to recover RCWs in the Ouachitas. Since I'm the smallest of the three, and newest on the job, I'm in the middle straddling the stick shift.

We've left Waldron before dawn because it's a long drive across Texas to the Kisatchie. It's my first long trip as a Forest Service employee and with Warren and Keith. Along the highway down in middle Texas, we max our speed because the schedule is tight for reaching the Kisatchie in time to trap woodpeckers at roost time. We're just charging down the road with radio in the background and the swoosh of big knobby off-road tires of our truck.

As we pass a Texas town, there's a big World War II field gun in front of a National Guard Armory. I make a casual joke that everyone ought to have a field gun in their front yard. Why did I say this? I don't know—probably because that's the sort of banal thing we discuss on campus. The whole country has been in a turmoil about the Brady Bill, which included restrictions on gun ownership.

"Can't be too protected," I add. On my right, Keith, a Vietnam vet, chuckles, but says nothing. I'm just talking, but as it turns out, I've inadvertently also thrown down a gauntlet. Warren is not slow to pick it up.

On my left, I can feel Warren twitch in his seat, and I can see that his face has reddened. "My father said you could tell the quality of a person by their views on the second amendment." He grips the steering wheel with his long fingers, but says nothing else. From the look on his face, I'm thinking the word "scowl" belongs here. No, not "scowl," it's way more than a scowl. Maybe thunderhead, with lots of lightning and thunder. This is my boss, and I've obviously pissed him off.

Here's where Keith could chime in with a joke. But my impression is that he is ooching closer to the door.

So here's just the right time for witty repartee, right? I'm a recent college grad, I have liberal opinions about the big issues, so I should have something bright to say. I remember that Bob Dole, the wounded World War II vet, conservative senator, and Republican senate leader during the Brady Bill debate, staked out a compromise position on the Brady debate.

"Well," I respond to Warren, "even Bob Dole thinks there are some reasonable limits on gun ownership." What I'm thinking about is that World War II cannon—surely every American doesn't need to own one, right?

Keith maintains his silence. Warren is beet red, the steering wheel clutched in an iron grip.

"Bob Dole is a damned communist," he says.

I sputter, halt and say, "Surely . . . you don't think Bob Dole is . . . ?"

I'm slow to realize what I've stepped into. Keith continues to sit, sphinxlike. Later he will tell me it was hot enough in the cab at that time, he thought he should jump and take his chances in the traffic. But now we're all silent. There's the radio again, and the tires, and the hard work ahead of trapping woodpeckers.

Warren has determined views on these issues, AND he is determined RCWs won't go extinct in the Ouachitas. This is Warren's trip and his idea to make the effort to move birds to save the Ouachita population.

By 1999–2000, the Ouachita RCW population had begun to grow. By 2011, the population had reached 145 adults with at least 56 nesting attempts. Trees in the forest were also getting older, a benefit to old-forest–loving woodpeckers.

I'm looking at a map of western Arkansas and eastern Oklahoma. There's a possible future here. Two populations of woodpeckers are involved: one managed by the Ouachita National Forest, the other by the Oklahoma Department of Wildlife Conservation. The first place we'll look is Waldron. It's mostly Scott County, homeland of the 155,000 acres of the Pine-Bluestem Project. Additions to the Ouachita project in Oklahoma bring the total to over 200,000 acres.

Now look at southeastern Oklahoma. Especially notice McCurtain County in the area around Broken Bow Lake. McCurtain County Wilderness Area, largest remaining tract of virgin shortleaf pine–hardwood habitat in the U.S., is on the north end of Broken Bow Lake. Woodpeckers are there as well. The woodpeckers seem aware they potentially occupy a huge landscape. A female banded in the McCurtain Wilderness in 1992 was found in Scott County in 1993. The distance was about 45.6 miles, if the bird had flown in a straight line. Three additional RCWs have made the same movement between eastern Oklahoma and western Arkansas. The whole region is part of the Ouachitas.

In 1995, a juvenile female was banded in Scott County, north of the Parks community. Subsequently, this bird "disappeared" from the Ouachita NF. However, Forest Service biologists in Louisiana, also working on RCW recovery, later spotted this same bird there—about 210 air miles away! This new Louisiana resident found a mate and nested, and reared several batches of young woodpeckers in the following years.

This event was incredible on several accounts. Chances that someone would actually find a bird that had flown this far is extremely low—

High quality Red-cockaded Woodpecker habitat, mainly with shortleaf pine and a recent prescribed burn, on Poteau Ranger District, Ouachita NF, in July 2007. Such habitat is also required by many other plant and animal species.

especially when you realize that this is one of the longest RCW dispersals ever recorded.

Early in 2005, an artificial RCW cavity became suddenly active in an area of the Ouachita NF north of Parks in Scott County. The band colors did not match those in use on the Ouachita NF. This bird had originated in Louisiana! It was not the original female RCW of 1995 either. Instead, it was her granddaughter who retraced the 210 air miles and took up residence on the Ouachita NF, two miles from where grandmother had started life.

My thinking is someday that daughter of mine Ariel, or perhaps her children may wish to again visit the old Kennedy and Neal home country. If she's interested, she may find there a landscape that serves numerous current human needs as well as supporting a species that was, in the long-ago days of her father's career, headed for extinction.

She may visit woodpeckers descended from those her old daddy knew in long ago years.

Young Red-tailed Hawk perched near the Craig State Fish Hatchery in Centerton, July 2006. Red-tails are the most common of the large hawks in western Arkansas. They come in a bewildering variety of colors, from light to dark, depending upon age and place of origin in North America.

Digiscoping Hawks and Eagles

IN MARCH, I'M twenty miles from home, one eye on the highway traffic. With the other eye I'm checking out oak barrens for nests. It's a busy highway, but I see something, find a place to pull off and get my spotting scope focused. That's an adult Great Horned Owl perched on its nest. Two white-downy owlets squirm below. The great yellow eyes and erect ear tufts are alert for crow intruders.

I didn't have a camera for taking bird pictures twenty-five years ago, but I do now—digital and with sufficient megapixels to collect an image through the 30-power telescope lens. This is called "digiscoping." I collect fifty images of the owl in a few minutes. My hope is that maybe five will be sharp enough to be interesting. Later, on my computer, I can do some editing. Saved as a JPEG file, the images can be shared via the Internet with anyone interested.

Here in western Arkansas, nests of Red-tailed Hawks and Great Horned Owls are often situated in a stout fork of gnarly oak trees—a mass of sticks below what will, after leaf out, become a green canopy. Woodlots hosting these nests are remnants of what nineteenth-century settlers called oak barrens or prairie barrens. Many of the trees date to the pioneer period. In other words, a two-hundred-year old tree is not a rarity in such places. Hawks and owls nest in the barrens and hunt open fields. It's a pattern several thousand years old.

Every town in western Arkansas is growing. We double, triple, then supersize into cities. This seems to necessitate cutting and bulldozing oak barrens. Former Tallgrass Prairies long ago converted to pastures now sport apartment complexes. And like nesting hawks and owls, people are starting families.

Yee Haw! Hold on to your horses and your Dodge Rams: more overbuilt homes and more overbuilt malls a'comin'.

When we find a stone artifact in the field, we know we have made contact with part of our past. It's the same with birds. They are relicts of a past life here, which remains intact, in part. Highway traffic and the development spurt tells me this will be the last year for this owl nest and likely for the oak barren itself. Red-tailed Hawks and Great Horned Owls have huge geographic ranges. Future nesting will occur further out from the thundering ring of development.

On a winter trip to Siloam Springs, I see an odd, white-looking hawk a quarter mile across a field near the airport. I pull off the road, set the scope in a window mount, and collect twelve digiscoped images before the bird flies. When I can't figure out what it is I've photographed, I e-mail the JPEG file to expert Brian Wheeler, author of *Raptors of Western North America*. We've never met in person, but I know from e-mails that he enjoys seeing raw hawk images captured in truly distant fields, like mine in northwest Arkansas. When he makes his call on the ID—it's a most likely a light morph of Harlan's Hawk—I have another piece of western Arkansas's natural history puzzle.

Welcome to the wide, wide and ever-changing world of modern technology. In this case, it's high-quality optics in a spotting scope and megapixels in an inexpensive camera. Welcome also to the wide, wide world of hawk watching through the finely crafted lens of a digital camera.

While working on a history of my family, I am amazed at old childhood photos of my mother's mother, whom I only knew in Fort Smith, Arkansas, as an older woman in a lot of pain, slowly dying of breast cancer. But I have photos of her as a young girl around 1910 on the porch of a farmhouse in the Ouachita Mountains. And later, in another image, there's my mother as a newborn in her arms, in 1917. The young girl has become a handsome woman in her twenties.

I bring this up because what I see when I'm birding is a lot like what I'm seeing in family pictures. Long-lived birds like hawks, eagles, and owls change a lot over a lifetime. Consider, for example, Red-tailed Hawks. Sure, considering their body shape and various plumage characteristics, they are noticeably red-tails throughout most of their long

Harlan's Hawk near Chensey Prairie Natural Area in January 2003. These big hawks nest in the far north and migrate into western Arkansas during the winter.

lives, but they also change. Unlike adults, juveniles don't sport the red tail. And, as things turn out, not all adults have the red tail. Some are mostly white, others pinkish, some streaked, some with bold tail feathers that illuminate red like stained glass during broad, lazy spirals against the sun.

People have different skin colors, body shapes, and sizes that started out mostly as adaptations to ecological realities. The same can be said about raptors. The red-tails from Alaska look different than Arkansas red-tails. It's a lot like humans from North America and Asia: one species, many superficial differences.

Winter is a golden opportunity to sharpen ID skills because many raptors winter here. The common big hawk is still our red-tail, the eastern form, *Buteo jamaicensis borealis*. When perched, it appears whitish underneath, but most have a noticeable dark "belly band." But in winter, our *borealis* is joined by a host of North American relatives. Some, like Harlan's Hawks, were once listed as separate species, but additional study indicated they were a localized form of red-tails, now identified as *Buteo jamaicensis harlani,* a subspecies.

Norman Wood's 1932 paper in *Wilson Bulletin* on Harlan's Hawk was largely based upon bird specimens collected in winter in Benton County, Arkansas. Wood was interested in the Audubon painting of a very black Harlan's Hawk that Audubon called a "black warrior." Our recent hawk watching confirms Wood's observations: Audubon's black warriors are fairly common in western Arkansas in winter.

The typical black warrior is a big raptor that's black or dark brown underneath, with dark wing linings and silvery primary flight feathers. This color pattern reminds me of a Turkey Vulture. Tails of black warriors vary a lot, based upon the subspecies involved. Some black warriors have reddish tails—these are probably western Red-tailed Hawks, *Buteo jamaicensis calurus,* migrating into western Arkansas from western North America. Others have tails whitish overall, with streaks and spots. These are Harlan's Hawks that nest in Alaska and extreme northwestern Canada.

Wood argued that Audubon had probably painted an immature *calurus* since its tail was "rather narrowly barred with blackish brown." And before we get too comfortable here, there are also "white warriors" including white-looking morphs of Harlan's Hawks and other red-tails, like Krider's Hawk, a pale morph of the usual *borealis* that migrates from its nesting grounds in the northern Great Plains. In their first winter season, "typical" red-tails also look pretty white. Plus, a large dark-looking raptor may not be any kind of a red-tail at all. It could be a dark morph Rough-legged Hawk, perhaps a juvenile Bald Eagle, or Golden Eagle.

And finally (well, not really), folks have recently been e-mailing me images made with their camera phones of a big white hawk out west of Fayetteville. This is maybe a leucistic red-tail? Or what?

Faced with numerous ID complications, we have several choices. All are valid responses to nature's complexities. Below are a randomly listed few:

> *JUST ENJOY.* Don't bother to buy all of the bird books. Don't purchase expensive binoculars and spotting scopes. Don't quit your job in order to get in more birding time. Just enjoy looking at birds and don't worry about having to attach Latin binomials and trinomials to everything seen.

Krider's Hawk, a big, white Red-tailed Hawk from the northern Great Plains that winters in Arkansas. This bird was near Gentry on February 3, 2011.

TRINOMIALIZE! Let no detail escape your eyes! Purchase ALL the identification books. Ramp up your birding equipment so you can clearly see that hawk perched a quarter of a mile away. Crank up your trusty high-value spotting scope to at least 60-power zoom. Compare that hawk with one of the two thousand illustrations in four books on the car seat next to you!

DIGISCOPE THAT HAWK. That is, get the hawk in focus through your scope just like you are a hunter sighting down the barrel of your trusty rifle. Your aim is true and the hawk falls, but only as an image now stored in the (hopefully robust) memory of your digital camera. The resulting image isn't Audubon's double elephant folio quality, but it's something to ponder at leisure, to compare to images in field guides. It's something to keep you warm at night, or keep your mind active while you're stalled in traffic somewhere . . . far from the hawks.

David Parker, a birder and an engineer, calls collecting images of birds in the field, "catch and release hunting."

The former Tallgrass Prairie region of northwestern Arkansas became an apple empire in the decades encompassing recovery from the Civil War to the end of World War I. Starting in the 1880s, a growing railroad network allowed fruit and related products to reach national markets. Between 1880 and 1900, roughly five million apple trees were planted in Washington and Benton counties. Orchards became a way for farmers to earn hard cash. In some respects, it was an experiment on a grand scale that eventually crashed because of a combination of killing frosts, unsettled markets, and codling moths and related insect problems. Final collapse came upon the opening of a superior apple-growing region in the state of Washington.

Traditionally, winter had been an idle time on farms, but around World War I some Benton County farmers raised winter chickens using small incubators and brooders. Edith Glover experimented with a portable brooder house that could be put in the yard on sunny days and taken up on the porch on cold days—something you can't do with an apple tree. Late spring frosts that destroyed entire fruit crops didn't faze Edith's brooder or the fat "Arkansas Quality" (AQ) chickens thus raised in winter.

Chicken flocks in the early years had run of the yard and the decaying orchard—doubtless a perfect opportunity for all chicken fanciers, including rat snakes, skunks, dogs, hawks, and owls.

There was many an Ozark momma who sent Number One son out in the yard to guard chickens, trusty rifle in hand. Needless to say, this guarding did not involve digiscoping. Son propped up in the welcoming shade of the barn and soon spotted a hawk perched in the post oak shading the chickens. Naturally, it was a Red-tailed Hawk, and naturally birds most frequently killed were these "chicken hawks," relatively slow-flying buteos skilled only at taking the slowest-moving prey. When compared to disease and weather, they had minimal impacts on the flocks but took the brunt of most of son's successful shots.

"Blue darters" (mostly Cooper's Hawks) made their lethal runs through these yards, but they don't often perch out in the open and were probably too fast and too wary for all but the truly crack shots among farm kids. The more progressive farmers also used traps baited with chickens and mounted on poles.

Whether shot or trapped, hawks and owls fell victim as the chicken empire grew in the orchard ruins. This is how many specimens later studied by Norman Wood were collected. One of those farm kids who guarded the early flocks was Maurice Loux, who lived four miles south of Maysville in Benton County.

Maysville is a pioneer and Civil War–era crossroads. It's still a crossroads for a few hundred folks on both sides of the Arkansas-Oklahoma state line. It's ten miles south of the Arkansas-Missouri line and less than an hour from Kansas. Its chief natural assets include grasslands and fertile soils of the historic Beatie Prairie. It's open and wind-swept, different than the mountainous Ozarks generally, especially the Boston Mountains south of Fayetteville.

When I met him at seventy, Maurice Loux was long retired from boyhood chores of guarding chicken flocks. Sure, he and spouse Theda Mae still raised a few birds, but these were for eggs and an occasional Sunday dinner. Their children were in the chicken business in a bigger way, just up the gravel road.

Mr. Loux was short and broad, with a ready smile. He's that guy on the farm tractor with weathered face, stocking cap, sunglasses, and several layers of chore clothes. Open, friendly, welcoming, talkative, Maurice was a lifelong resident of the farm where he lived. He was also a retired schoolteacher and published historian of Maysville and Benton County. Born in 1913, he was old enough to remember the fruit empire and the last of the Greater Prairie-Chickens around Maysville.

Poultry production had taken a big upswing at Maysville in the late 1970s. Just within a one-and-a-half-mile radius of the Loux farm, 350,000 chickens were being raised every eight weeks by the 1980s. Dead chickens were removed from the houses every day. More birds going to market meant an upswing in more dead birds for disposal. Generally, the dead birds were spread out in a pasture or in an out-of-sight dump in a back-field fencerow. Here they provided food for Red-tailed Hawks, crows, vultures, coyotes, and other scavengers. Wintering eagles also took note.

Loux saw the first Bald Eagle on his farm in 1979, a single bird that remained most of the winter. He saw 4 in 1980, 19 in 1981, 33 in 1982, 51 in 1983, and 74 in 1984. Doug James and I would tally 115 birds in the Maysville area by 1985.

A mature Bald Eagle perched in an ice-encrusted oak tree near Gravette, January 20, 2007. Bald Eagles are a familiar sight during the winter months in western Benton County, and a little ice and snow doesn't deter them.

The eagles weren't just feeding on chickens. Large dead chickens were only available every few weeks. Loux told outdoor writer Joe Mosby that his eagles were also foraging on the afterbirth of cattle on farms throughout the area. "I've heard all the old tales about eagles killing grown cows and carrying off young calves. But I have never seen them bother a calf, even a newborn one. They'll walk right up beside it and eat the afterbirth but never bother the calf."

In 1985, a Northwest Arkansas Audubon Society eagle-watching event was welcomed on the Loux farm. January 19 dawned cold and windy and got colder as the day proceeded. Mr. Loux used his farm tractor to gather up several bucket loads of dead chickens as eagle bait. A crowd of 130 Auduboners and friends met nearby in Decatur and formed a carpool for the drive to Maysville. In the Loux's front yard—and convenient for freezing eagle-watchers—the local 4-H club raised money by selling doughnuts, coffee, and hot chocolate. Eventually, at least fifty Bald Eagles rampaged through the dead chickens. A reporter for the *Morning News* in Springdale summarized the scene as follows:

As eagle watchers stared at the birds through binoculars and spotting scopes, an eagle waltzed through a smorgasbord of dead poultry, seemingly looking for just the right chicken to provide a satisfying lunch. As the raptor scrutinized the menu, another eagle swooped down, grabbed a chicken, and flew to a nearby tree, clutching the deceased chicken in his talons—sort of like it had just visited the drive-up window.

But it didn't seem to matter to those gathered that the eagles weren't perched on a limb jutting from a majestic cliff in one of our national parks with the Star Spangled Banner playing in the background. People were seeing eagles and seeing them close up.

Northwest Arkansas Audubon's Kathy Hall wrote, "A highlight of the morning was the release by Vivian and Joe Stockton of a Red-tailed Hawk that had recovered from an injury. It flew swiftly away from the crowd. Unlike everyone else, it didn't seem the least bit inclined to stop and admire the eagles."

In the middle of all the action is Maurice Loux, in bib overalls and sunglasses. He wears his heavy work shirts, a warm work cap. He has binoculars, but these hang unused from his left arm as he shares eagle tales with Auduboners, Cub Scouts, the 4-H group, and reporters. No more hawk shooting now that chickens are all raised in barns, he says. He sure liked hawks and eagles a lot more in 1985 than he did when he was a kid.

Any season is reason enough for hawk-watching expeditions. We like birding the open country, but we retain enough of what's called "the Protestant ethic" to know it needs to look like work if we are going to pursue our pleasure seriously. Otherwise, it will seem that we are goofing off. Generally speaking, we have a mission in mind.

For example, where are northwest Arkansas's American Kestrels during the breeding season? Finding these open-country birds requires us to check big grasslands in April or May—months when local kestrels can be nesting. There are kestrels at the U of A farm in Fayetteville, on the old Norwood prairie along Highway 16 west of Wedington, and on a half-dozen old prairies scattered around Benton County. We can expand to the old prairies in Madison County—Hindsville comes to mind—and in spots like Baker Prairie Natural Area at Harrison. There

This American Kestrel perches on a power pole while it surveys the open country north of Maysville on December 2, 2010.

will be kestrels in all of these areas. When the day is done, we'll have accomplished our mission.

What are the typical fall arrival and spring departure dates for Harlan's Hawk? Finding and identifying them will provides excuses enough for long days in both October and early April. And in the post Maurice Loux era, are there still Bald Eagles in numbers at Maysville and Gentry? And how about that big eagle communal roost? These questions provide a suitable mission in mid-December or anytime in January.

Kim Smith and I had another mission in 1983. We shared an office together at the University of Arkansas that year. I was working on a bird book, and Kim was teaching ornithology for Doug James, who was in Nepal on a Fulbright Fellowship. It began to snow on December 20 and snow turned into an ice storm on December 21. The temperature fell to minus seven the following day, and remained there, more or less, into the New Year.

A sharp cold snap with ice and snow pushes birds into Arkansas that typically winter further to the north or west. For example, there are

Common Mergansers at Lake Fayetteville on December 22—a rare bird in northwest Arkansas. At the University of Arkansas farm there are at least three flocks of Horned Larks and Lapland Longspurs totaling over two hundred birds—we usually see none or maybe a dozen or so. The Arkansas River is iced over.

December 27 proves a star-studded day when winter ice yields avian treasures. Kim and I tour northwest Arkansas: Siloam Springs, Gentry, Highfill, Springtown, and visit several reservoirs and an airport. By the end of the day we've found two western Red-tailed Hawk "black warriors," six Harlan's Hawks, and fifty-seven other Red-tailed Hawks and seen 180 Mallards standing on ice; and most exciting of all, three light-plumaged Rough-legged Hawks, for Arkansas still a record number almost thirty years later.

Research doesn't always require subzero weather. One perennially nagging ornithological issue in Arkansas involves the nesting status of Swainson's Hawk, a fairly common bird in the western United States that always excites us when we see them in Arkansas, where they are rare. On July 27, 2002, Mike Mlodinow, Rob Doster, and I conduct a casual census in Benton County.

Our first Swainson's is soaring north of the Flint Creek power plant. We find a second bird in the old Wet Prairie area north of Maysville. Most tantalizing, we watch a bird carrying a rodent near the intersection of Game Farm and Leonard Ranch east of Maysville. For a few moments we think we've found a nest. The bird seems headed toward an oak barren nearby.

Ticks and chiggers are real bad here in July. I keep thinking either Mike or Rob will just bail out and take off through the field toward the trees. They too are tick and chigger vets. We have all been wounded and subsequently made wiser by warm season insect skirmishes and subsequent nights of infernal itching.

We follow that Swainson's Hawk with our binoculars, feet planted firmly on the insect-free gravel road. Didn't find a nest—boo! Didn't get any chigger bites—yea!

My friend Irene Camargo and I have been out on a few casual bird walks. She has prepared a manuscript for a book titled *Gawk at the Hawk*.

As an undergrad at LSU she was a student of renowned birder and mammalogist George Lowery. His name and reputation I recognize from his classic *Louisiana Birds*. Irene's apartment is lighted in part by an owl lamp hand-painted by her mother. There are bird images on her walls and feeders outside her windows.

A career teacher, she has lived most of her fifty years in the south: Louisiana, Texas, Oklahoma, and Arkansas. But when she speaks, I hear in her voice more than a hint of her White Plains, New York, birth, her mother Veronica's unabashed Queens accent, and her father Mario's Latin origins. He is a native of Columbia and descendant of Spanish carpenters who built the Pinta, Nina, and Santa Maria of Columbus fame.

Irene's serious about teaching and what follows, grading student papers. They're piled on couch, table, and at end of the fall semester, spilling onto the rug. She's taking a break. I have been invited for dinner.

A hawk-watching trip, I volunteer, might provide ideas about illustrations suitable for *Gawk*. Could she maybe take off a few extra hours on Saturday? Couldn't she use a break from grading? She studies my proposal while eyeing lab reports due back to her students on Tuesday. Fingering the reports, she thinks aloud. Well, I can work on Saturday, maybe finish on Monday. Her shoulder-length brown hair flips around, and I catch a few silver streaks there as sun pours through her front window—goldfinches at a feeder hanging there. She turns toward me, something brewing in her brown eyes.

Suddenly, her hand darts out. I'm grabbed in the ribs. GAWWWWK AT THE HAWWWWK, she shrieks. Would Sunday be OK?

Irene is from a Catholic family of four girls, four boys. She has lots of nieces and nephews. Friends from Louisiana to Oklahoma have kids. Her book is for children. The lab reports will wait her return from a long day afield in the old prairie country.

I will provide car, digital camera, spotting scope, and the focus down to the last, bitter trinomial. She will provide healthy snacks, filtered water, humor, warmth, and the *raison d'etre* for our day: field studies of hawks. We will gawk at hawks, owls, eagles, and whatever comes our way.

We draw a cool clear sunny day—down to near zero last night and a blush of snow on the ground this morning, but warming. We've headed out west from Fayetteville on Highway 412. As we cross through the

Illinois River bottoms we can see last year's stick nests of Great Blue Herons near the tops of still leafless sycamores—and one Great Blue perched there.

At Siloam Springs we turn onto Airport Road. Out in the fields paralleling the runway there are flocks of Horned Larks—maybe 250 of them, plus Lapland Longspurs, Savannah Sparrows, and lots of meadowlarks.

Meadowlarks: most are Easterns, but often there are a few Westerns, too.

A dark *buteo* is perched on a round hay bail. In the crisp light it's apparent the overall dark plumage is marked with blotchy white patches. Big bluestem grass partly obscures the bird. The digiscoped image is somewhat blurred because the camera keeps metering the grass. Studying the image at home later will convince me this is Harlan's Hawk.

Irene spots an American Kestrel in the pioneer cemetery north of the airport. This bird surveys the big landscape and basically ignores us. It's on her side of the car. We hold our breath in hopes. We quietly join the spotting scope with a window tripod mount. Irene takes the camera and deftly digiscopes images of this kestrel perched on one foot, spotted breast feathers puffed against the morning cold. This little falcon's brilliant plumage is illuminated by brilliant light.

Then we are off to the Eagle Watch Nature Trail near Gentry in Benton County, where we see eight Bald Eagles perched in one tree (a digiscopable scene) and fifteen eagles visible from the observation deck. In addition, there are thirty Green-winged Teal on the lake. Among two red-tails seen there is an intriguing bird that, in the morning winter light, looks chocolate brown. It's a long ways away, but we collect an image with the aid of the scope's 30-power eyepiece.

Now we decide to circle back toward Chesney Prairie Natural Area, always good in winter for hawks. The drive is along Highway 59, which thunders with chicken truck traffic. The highway crosses Flint Creek in a large wooded bottomland, and there I spot a Barred Owl dead on the roadside. Little damage is visible—feathers forming breast bars are immaculate, the facial disk feathers and "mustache" equally so. It's easy to imagine those big brown eyes wide open and staring. After a quick look, I'm ready to move the carcass into the woods and drive on, but Irene isn't.

She carefully picks the bird up and as carefully carries it to the woods. Slightly shielded from the highway, she sits and studies the tail, wings, and big puffy head. As I watch, I suddenly remember that she is, after all, a biologist, and a teacher of anatomy and physiology. But there is a lot more than science involved.

This owl encompasses in its existence the spirit of forested river bottoms. Its lethal impact with mechanized modernity barreling up and down Highway 59 is telling. Irene seems oblivious to the roaring traffic and the fact that I'm half back to the car. Only half, though, because her care gives me pause for thinking about my own quickness to name the bird and move on. I sense that I am missing something. Irene respectfully covers the bird with leaves and twigs.

On a gravel road near Chesney Prairie Natural Area we spot a bird perched high in a big snag. The view leaves a lot to be desired because the sun is behind it. It's on Irene's side. Kestrel is my first thought, but it doesn't look quite right. We are a ways off, and there's the sun, and I am scrunched down and looking past Irene. She is plastered against her seat, allowing me the view. When we get the scope mounted on the window, it's obvious it's no kestrel. But what? A Peregrine?

My hands are shaking as I realize we have a rare, rare SOMETHING. But what? I get the camera up to the scope and squeeze off three images before the bird flies—not even realizing at this point that I've nearly crushed Irene, victim of my excitement, my Hail Mary lunge for her window—and without time for sharp focus on the scope. We pile out of the car in hopes of a better look. No luck. Back in the car, I review three images.

Back lighting from the sun has cruelly eliminated some detail, creating a not very helpful artistic aurora behind the bird. But also, there in the images are the strong mustache mark and the obvious start of dark feathers in the axillary area. These are not *Birding* cover images. However, the focus is close enough and camera smart enough to document a PRAIRIE FALCON—an extremely rare bird in Arkansas. I am beside myself with joy. It's time to dance the birder's victory jig.

We have time enough for another stop, and this one will be at Chesney proper. We have a clear sunny afternoon with rising temperatures. Right there where we park there are maybe five Red-tailed

This Prairie Falcon, a very rare bird in Arkansas, perched momentarily on a snag near Chesney Prairie Natural Area on January 17, 2003, just long enough to permit collection of a few digiscoped images.

Hawks. Two are especially gorgeous with dark outlines and bright red tails, flying in low circles. I move from the red-tails to what for me is bigger quarry: scanning sky and treetops for a big falcon.

Out of the car, away from the scope and camera, Irene is silent and meditative. She lays down on her back in the grass, arms and legs outstretched. Eyes closed, she sky bathes, luxuriating in the great winged creatures ruling its broad dominion.

I was up in Benton County again last winter and not far from the Loux place. There are still eagles up there, sometimes quite a few. I got caught up in a reverie about that big day in 1985 when we had the eagle party. I drove down Loux Road to the old farmhouse where we had so much enjoyed conversations with Maurice and his family.

I knew Maurice had passed away in 1997, but the house and yard still looked about the same. There were tended bird feeders. Theda Mae survived until 2004, and the place was now home to their daughter Carol who also treasured memories from the big eagle days.

Just like old times, I was invited into the living room. We were soon looking at scrapbooks and photo albums of eagles and eagle watchers. Carol mentioned something else I might like to see. She disappeared for a moment into another room, and came out with a big quilt. Theda Mae was a quilter—something I'd forgotten.

This quilt—her last one—was covered with birds.

Pictured in back is the much-coveted Yellow-billed Loon. In front is the smaller and more numerous Common Loon. Tenkiller Lake in northeastern Oklahoma, Janaury 27, 2010.

Yellow-billed Loon

I'M NOT A loon expert, even after thirty years of bird watching. But I'm really interested. Loons got into my blood in the early 1970s. I was deeply fascinated by *The Horn Island Logs of Walter Inglis Anderson*. He studied, drew, painted, and wrote about the natural history of his native Gulf Coast. This book included his drawings and painting of numerous birds on the Gulf Coast, including loons. In the late 1970s, I followed up that interest with several trips to Walter Anderson's country. I saw for myself big rafts of wintering loons off Horn Island. They have occupied my mind and spirit since.

Loons don't nest in Arkansas. We are too far south. But many migrate south to the Gulf Coast and they overwinter on larger artificial lakes all over Arkansas. The chance to see loons here is one of the attractions of winter. And of course, we especially like to see the ones that are rare here: Red-throated, Pacific, and especially Yellow-billed Loon.

I may be trapped in my Fayetteville home by a winter storm, but in my mind I see loons. They are far out on the cold waters of a lake in the Ozark Mountains, forested hills rising above. Loons survey the scene above the water where I also watch, then survey what I don't see, head in the water. With a bare ripple, they disappear and swim underwater after fish.

I see a raft of six loons on a field trip to Beaver Lake dam, near Eureka Springs northeast of Fayetteville. Cold weather keeps the bass boats with their noisy powerful engines in the marina. Mostly, it's just me and loons. What I hear far out on the lake are deep moans, barks, and an occasional yodel. There isn't much other sound in midwinter. Loons own the lake and on such days, my full attention.

At fifty-four miles northeast of Fayetteville, Beaver is a little closer to home. But a good day on Beaver involves half-dozen loons. So news from northeastern Oklahoma was astonishing. Back in the late 1980s, Oklahoma birders Jeri McMahon and Jimmy Norman discovered high numbers of Common Loons on Lake Tenkiller in northeastern Oklahoma. They counted 120 in just part of the lake on March 30, 1989. Tenkiller is eighty miles southwest of Fayetteville, an easy and picturesque drive through the rural Ozarks straddling western Arkansas and eastern Oklahoma.

On February 17, 1990, Fayetteville birder Mike Mlodinow joined McMahon and Norman in counting 133 loons at Tenkiller. McMahon published these findings in the *Bulletin of the Oklahoma Ornithological Society* (March 1991). Mike was also checking Beaver Lake. He never found big concentrations, but on November 17, 1991, he identified a Yellow-billed Loon near the Beaver Lake dam site. It is one of only two records for Arkansas.

With my interest in birds, I could have been right on top of these loon developments. Instead, I was blissfully unaware. Like many other new parents, my life was being reorganized. My daughter Ariel was five in 1990, around the time things started happening at Tenkiller. With a new daughter came new responsibilities. I was in graduate school as loon fever spread through the birding community from the Tenkiller incubus. My new job was to learn all I could about an endangered bird, the Red-cockaded Woodpecker, so that I could join in U.S. Forest Service efforts to bring it back from the brink of extinction. This is a way of saying my life had changed, and loons didn't register. I was barely passing a statistics class that fall when Mike discovered his loon at Beaver Lake.

I went off to the magnificent shortleaf pine forests and Red-cockaded Woodpeckers of the Ouachita National Forest after graduate school. I didn't make it over to Tenkiller. I didn't get to see Mike's loon. But seeds were sown.

I didn't see much of the local birding community during the first decade of my Forest Service career. It was all about woodpeckers and all about trying to figure out how to combine a professional career with being a responsible father. However, my course was again reset in 2002. Mike had found Henslow's Sparrow in the summer of 2001, right in Fayetteville. The presence of this rare bird in town was stunning. Mike and I and a few others made a concentrated effort to find out more. We

Left to right: Mike Mlodinow, Rose Ann Barnhill, Andrea Green, and Rob Doster scanning Rocky Branch on Beaver Lake for loons, November 2002.

also found them nearby in another field. I got involved in ultimately futile efforts to protect the habitat from commercial development.

Tenkiller State Park has been hosting "loon watch" field trips since 2001. It was not only Common Loons that were being seen. Folks were finding the other three species: Red-throated, Pacific, and most amazing of all, Yellow-billed Loon. My daughter Ariel was now a teenager in high school. Increasingly, I divided my time between my Forest Service career and life in Fayetteville, including more involvement with local birding. I had graduated from looking for Henslow's Sparrows to more general birding trips that I had no time for in more than ten years.

On February 7, 2004, Mike, David Parker, and I went over to Kerr Dam on the Arkansas River to look for gulls, then north to Tenkiller. The horde of gulls at Kerr Dam included Ringed-billed, Bonaparte's, and Herring Gulls, and a single spectacular Glaucous Gull. All were in a swirling or floating mass below the dam, with a mixture of a couple of thousand Double-crested Cormorants and maybe four hundred white pelicans. The wind had come up by the time we got to Tenkiller. The lake was mostly whitecaps, but there were many loons. Near the end of the day, with daylight fading, we set up our scopes at the tip of the Strayhorn area, checking the big open waters to the north.

Mike picked out a bird at some distance and commenced to study it. "I think I've got the loon," he said. Parker and I lined up to see what he had found: a brownish bird, with a light-colored and consistently uptilted bill. The possibility that it might be an immature-plumage Common Loon was quickly eliminated. It was the coveted Yellow-billed. The bird in Mike's scope was for me the flowering of seeds sown in the late 1980s.

January 27, 2010: This winter's Yellow-billed Loon at Tenkiller got on the grapevine a couple of weeks ago when Sandy Berger, a birder from Fort Smith, heard about it from some Oklahomans who'd seen it and photographed it at the state park. Looking at those photographs reminded me of that day years ago when I was sitting in my Forest Service office and read in the paper about the Tenkiller State Park loon watches. I couldn't just up and walk out of my office for it then. But now I'm retired from the Forest Service. I can go and look for that loon myself. Right now!

OK, I just have to say it here: isn't it kinda loonie to go racing eighty miles away in the dead of winter? For a loon?

Today I am up early. The wind chimes that hang outside my bedroom are silent. There's promise in the silence of wind chimes. No wind could mean a good day when the water is smooth. There won't be white caps that make it really tough to see far away bird blobs bobbing up and down, up and down, and out of sight. But we have a sleet-ice-snow storm coming tonight. So I'm thinking I'm about to lose my chance for Tenkiller and THAT loon. I want the close, knowing view—to really take it in, to occupy so far as it is reasonable the Yellow-billed Loon experience—whatever that is. It's an undefined quantity for me, perhaps also unknowable. But I know I want it. I can't think of any legitimate reason not to go. Well . . . there is that carbon footprint issue: a lot of driving, a lot of carbon released into the atmosphere. I silently ask forgiveness. Tenkiller here I come.

I've covered those eighty miles in predawn darkness. I'm at Tenkiller at 7:30, head right out to Fisherman's Point, and spend an hour trying for the loon. Common Loons are numerous and some are calling. With eyeball screwed to the scope eyepiece, I scan Common Loon to Common Loon. Finally, I have it, but again way, way off, like the loon from 2004: too far to satisfy.

The solution is to leave Fisherman's Point, drive the three miles of Pine Cove Road that winds its way toward a campground called Shady Grove. It looks to me like THE loon is fishing in the lake just beyond a sandstone bluff line below the campground. Pine Cove Road is blocked half way to Shady Grove. I park, grab my spotting scope and camera, duck under the gate, and take off up the road, across the campground, down through viney woods.

There, among the big sandstone blocks, is a fine view of the lake. AND lo, the Yellow-billed Loon.

As I watch the loon I think what a long journey it's been. I've come from afar. I don't mean eighty miles. Thirty years ago I was deeply thrilled by Walter Anderson's creative and inspiring observations of nature. It's a long ways from my Forest Service office twenty years ago, working on rare Red-cockaded Woodpeckers, when at the same time folks first began to find Tenkiller's amazing winter loons. It's almost twenty years since Mike discovered a Yellow-billed Loon on Beaver Lake that I didn't get to see because I was helping raise Ariel and at the same time trying to pass a statistics course that had me completely over the barrel.

Here, below Shady Grove, it's finally me and the Yellow-billed Loon, close up. There's a Pacific Loon too, plus many Common Loons. I watch loons and feel the years are in focus. I see the loon clearly and collect some images through my spotting scope, a souvenir of the day. It's peaceful among the rocks alongside Lake Tenkiller where loons are diving for fish, calling quietly back and forth. It's good to have a time, even a brief time, when the years come into focus.

What is it about the loon? I'm trying to figure this out.

Partly, it's the excitement of novelty, a local rarity. Yellow-billed Loons in the south are celebrities in the birding community. Thinking about all of this takes me back to 1991, when Mike found his loon. Bragging rights accrue to discovery—viewing, photo-izing rare birds. No such excitement accrues to Common Loons. In our inland,

American White Pelicans below Kerr Dam on the Arkansas River on February 7, 2004.

mountainous region, Yellow-billed Loons are pure exotics. It's a long ways from the Arctic to northeastern Oklahoma and northwestern Arkansas. There was a time when spices from the Orient aroused all western Europe. Yellow-billed Loons are rare and intriguing spices in our age of environmental consciousness.

Perhaps this bird is special because of the challenge (and hoped-for reward) in finding it in twelve thousand acres of water. It's the challenge of discerning its features from others that are similar, like immature Common Loons. In this respect, looking for the Yellow-billed Loon may be something of an athletic event, jumping hurdles and crossing the finishing line with milliseconds to spare, bird scored against long odds.

Far away, on a big lake, loons can look like gray amorphous lumps and make no obvious impression, especially for folks not infected by loon fever. Looking at them through a spotting scope on a cold day is an acquired taste. But if you get yourself all secreted among the bushes and rocks of the shoreline, and stay quiet and still, the loon flotillas casually drift close. There's chance for an eye-to-eye. These great creatures look calm and knowing. They peer into the water, and in this act they inspect a hidden universe. Then with a modest ripple, they timelessly disappear.

When I see loons it's like I'm wandering in geological time. They look like the ancient diving seabirds *Hesperornis* from the Cretaceous period—just for the sake of discussion, say 65 million years ago. Their bodies were roughly like those of modern loons. And like our loons, they chased fish underwater. I look at distant loons and wonder if we're back in a vast Cretaceous sea? Is that *Hesperornis* out there? A birdwatcher from 2010 seeking a Yellow-billed Loon comes eye-to-eye with the earth's ancient secrets. I feel amazed and wonderfully lost. The concerns of 2010 seem to dissipate: trucks in the background, airplanes overhead, disappointments, my carbon footprint. Time, evolution, and emotion compress into a moment lacking temporal dimension. Like I said earlier, it's good to have a time, even a brief time, when the years come into focus.

Maybe it's just the fascination that comes from a good hearing of all those barks, croaks, moans, and yodels. What are they saying? It sounds like conversation. It reminds me of *seep* notes among Savannah Sparrows in big grassy fields and all of that peeping among White-throated Sparrows as they go to roost in the evening. What are the creatures saying? Is any of it for us? Do they offer praise for the day, or are they just jostling for the best overnight perch, the best fish? Loon sounds drift over the waters of a huge lake, snug in the Ozark hills, far from the north country where they nest.

Thirty years ago I was trying to understand bare essentials about birds and the environment. I have managed to learn a lot, especially as it pertains to northwestern Arkansas. More recently I have begun to see more of the world through the eyes of birds, metaphorically speaking. I don't mean this as a bunch of anthropomorphic clap-trap. I'm not claiming to have become "one with the loons." I mean this more in the way of that dimensionless aspect that isn't very well described in our physical world of careers, clocks, appointments, possessions, and projects.

Seeing loons rates as purely exotic compared to the average humdrum plainness of most of my days. Pursuing and finding a rare Yellow-billed Loon is excitement, an intoxicant. It's exploring off into uncharted space. Has anyone really been here before?

In winter, we live on loon planet. On a special day, with a little luck, we may see the Yellow-billed Loon.

JOSEPH C. NEAL is a native of western Arkansas. He is the author of *The Birdside Baptist*, co-author of *Arkansas Birds* (with Douglas A. James). For the *History of Washington County Arkansas*, he wrote the historical sections that provide background for the book's family stories. He has worked as a biologist for three decades, including seventeen years in the USDA Forest Service as a wildlife biologist working to restore the endangered Red-cockaded Woodpecker in the Ouachita Mountains. Now retired from the Forest Service, he continues his Arkansas bird studies from his home in Fayetteville. He is active in both the Arkansas Audubon Society and the Northwest Arkansas Audubon Society, where he serves as field-trip leader. He writes and records commentaries for *Ozarks at Large*, a feature on KUAF, a local National Public Radio affiliate. He is a visiting scholar in the University of Arkansas's Department of Biological Sciences and writes a local bird column for the *Washington County Observer*.

Photo by Joan Reynolds

www.ingramcontent.com/pod-product-compliance
Lightning Source LLC
Chambersburg PA
CBHW032112090426
42743CB00007B/326